Epilepsy, Psychiatry and Learning Difficulty

Tim Betts, FRCPsych
Senior Lecturer in Psychiatry
Birmingham University
Consultant Neuropsychiatrist
South Birmingham Mental Health Trust
Birmingham Brainwave and Peter Jeavons
Neurophysiology Unit
Queen Elizabeth Psychiatric Hospital
Birmingham B15 2QZ
United Kingdom

President, International League Against Epilepsy, British Branch
Honorary Medical Advisor, British Epilepsy Association

Sponsored by an educational grant from Parke-Davis
Over fifty years of experience in the management of epilepsy

In memory of Peter Jeavons

Whose wise counsels imbue this work: everything I still value in the practice of epilepsy medicine and psychiatry I learnt from him.

Dedication

Dedicated to the two teams in my life: my wife and children, Pam, Hannah, Victoria, George, Florence and Tim, who make it such a pleasure to come home; and my colleagues at Birmingham Brainwave, Kate Smith, Kate Rudd, Cathy Fox, Clare Cook, Marilyn Hardman, Lynn Howes and Megan Brady, whose loyalty, industry and cheerfulness add so much to the working day.

The opinions expressed in this book are those of the author and do not necessarily reflect the views of Parke-Davis.

© Martin Dunitz Ltd 1998

First published in the United Kingdom in 1998 by

Martin Dunitz Ltd
The Livery House
7– 9 Pratt Street
London NW1 0AE

A CIP record for this book is available from the British Library.

ISBN 1-85317-616-8

Printed and bound in Italy.

Contents

Introduction

'Epilepsy is important to the psychiatrist and the psychiatrist is important to epilepsy.'

In certain branches of psychiatry (neuropsychiatry, old age psychiatry, child psychiatry and learning disability psychiatry) a thorough knowledge of epilepsy, its recognition and management is essential: but knowledge of it is important to all psychiatrists, even those working in psychiatric disciplines apparently remote from organic diseases, like psychotherapy.

However much disputed and controversial, there are links between certain forms of mental illness and epilepsy itself and epilepsy enters into the differential diagnosis of sudden paroxysmal changes in behaviour, thinking and feeling, which are the bread and butter of psychiatry.

Psychiatrists in any discipline are going to see more people with epilepsy than would be expected by chance: even if they choose to leave the medical care of the patient to another specialist they must know enough about the modern investigation and management of epilepsy to be able to understand the process of diagnosis and treatment and the effect that modern anticonvulsants have on the brain and the psyche. The modern management of epilepsy should very much involve itself with the social and psychological management of the patient as well as the purely medical. The psychiatrist should recognize that epilepsy has been over medicalized and that there is a growing interest in the psychological management of seizures themselves. Epilepsy teaches us much about how physical and psychological factors intermingle in the brain and that it is as important to understand the mind of someone with epilepsy as it is to understand that person's brain structure or function.

In the field of learning disability knowledge of epilepsy is essential, particularly because its recognition and management is often difficult. It is easy to further impair already imperilled brain function in the pursuit of controlling seizures: although often difficult to obtain it is particularly necessary in the learning disabled person with epilepsy to ensure that full investigation has preceded decisions about treatment. What follows is an attempt to inform the psychiatrist about the salient features of the diagnosis and management of epilepsy and highlight those aspects of epilepsy most important to the practice of psychiatry. This is why, for instance, the section on aetiology concentrates on those

aspects important to learning disability psychiatrists (e.g. tuberous sclerosis) or on the causes of seizures, the importance of which have only recently been acknowledged following the development of high quality MRI scanning and which may not be well known to psychiatrists.

Likewise the psychological aspects of treatment, at least as important as the physical, will be emphasized as they are often neglected in neurologically based texts.

Radiological and EEG material used to illustrate the text is drawn from the clinical practice of Birmingham Brainwave and I am grateful to the radiographers and radiologists of the Birmingham Nuffield Hospital and the Queen Elizabeth Hospital, Birmingham and to the Peter Jeavons Neurophysiology Unit for preparing the EEG illustrations. Linda Keating deserves warm thanks for her help in preparing this text.

Further reading
Betts T (1993) Neuropsychiatry. In: *A Textbook of Epilepsy* (eds J Laidlaw, A Richens and D Chadwick) Edinburgh: Churchill Livingstone, pp.397–457.

Epilepsy: basic mechanisms

An epileptic seizure is a sudden, paroxysmal, synchronous and repetitive discharge of cerebral neurons, the observable and reportable clinical symptoms of the attack depending on where the discharge started, how far it has spread and, to some extent, how long it went on for. Seizure discharges in eloquent areas of the brain may produce a distorted pastiche of the function of that part of the brain (e.g. focal movement) or may interrupt function in that area so that normal processes cannot take place (e.g. speech arrest). Epileptic seizures are usually self limiting (specific inhibiting mechanisms exist in the brain), may be provoked (e.g. by flickering light) but usually appear to be spontaneous (although there is a growing body of thought that believes that many seizures are provoked in some way). A person has *epilepsy* if they show a recurrent tendency to have seizures. Epileptic seizures in an individual tend to be stereotyped and are, usually, brief.

Knowledge of the basic mechanisms comes from animal work but it is assumed that it can be extrapolated to human epilepsy and some human evidence is now available, both from material obtained at operation and by direct measurement prior to surgery.[1]

Epileptic activity starts at a cellular level; epileptic activity spreads to *cellular aggregates* which discharge repeatedly and in synchrony so that the epileptic activity *propagates*. In the single cell epileptic activity is marked by the paroxysmal depolarizing shift (PDS) **(Figure 1)** in which there is a sudden brief depolarization of the cell membrane with fast and slow action potentials (mediated by sodium and calcium ions respectively).

Neuronal aggregates develop repetitive *synchronous* firing probably through excitatory synaptic connections (other mechanisms may

be involved). The summation of their electrical activity can be recorded (providing they are near enough and generate sufficient activity) in the surface EEG as the interictal spike and wave **(Figure 1)**. The *spike* coincides with an increased likelihood of individual neurons firing (summation of excitatory impulses) and the *wave* with reduced likelihood of neurons firing (summation of inhibitory impulses).

Seizure propagation to other neuronal aggregates in remote areas of the brain (or even to the entire neuronal pool) is along facilitated

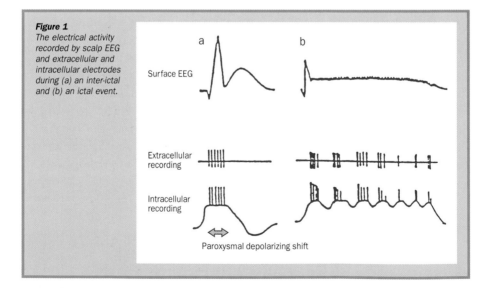

Figure 1
The electrical activity recorded by scalp EEG and extracellular and intracellular electrodes during (a) an inter-ictal and (b) an ictal event.

a   b

Surface EEG

Extracellular recording

Intracellular recording

Paroxysmal depolarizing shift

pathways but other mechanisms may exist as well: if sufficient activity is generated there may even be a direct electrical field effect.

The initiation, continuation and suppression of epileptic activity is mediated by mechanisms that increase either excitation or inhibition (see Tables 1 and 2), glutamate being the main excitatory transmitter and GABA (gamma-aminobutyric acid) the main inhibitory one. The GABAA receptor is important in epilepsy and also relates to the benzodiazepine receptor which has three classes of receptor ligands, agonists, antagonists and inverse agonists: agonists facilitate the GABAA receptor and are *anticonvulsant*, inverse agonists are *convulsant*. The benzodiazepine receptor (and the drugs that influence it) is important to psychiatry, and can be regarded as the receptor that mediates the stress response.

Seizure activity may cause changes in neurons, even cell death, through influx of calcium ions (due to excessive glutamate release — similar to mechanisms that occur in acute brain trauma or stroke); drugs that inhibit pathological glutamate release may be neuroprotective. Chronic cell changes (both chemical and structural) take place after even a

Table 1
Ions in epilepsy.

Excitatory	Inhibitory
Na^+	Mg^{++}
Ca^{++}	Cl^-
	K^+

Table 2
Transmitters and receptors important in epilepsy.

Excitatory	Inhibitory
Glutamate	Gamma-aminobutyric acid (GABA)
N-Methyl-D-aspartate (NMDA)	
Kainate	Benzodiazepine

single seizure with loss of fibres and neurons and disorganization of synapses and 'sprouting' of fibres leading to secondary changes in neuronal excitability. These changes may explain why epileptic seizures become self reinforcing and emphasize the need to control seizures quickly once epilepsy has started. Eventually, we will understand epilepsy at a molecular genetic level, and rapid strides are being made in this direction.

A model of the propagation of epileptic activity in the brain based on a primate model of epileptogenesis has particular relevance to the psychiatrist.[2] In her study of the spread of epileptic activity Lockard described the Group 1 epileptogenic cells, situated in the centre of the discharging focus, which were chronically firing in an epileptic mode (*pacemaker cells*). Group II epileptogenic cells surrounded the Group I cells and were capable of firing either in the epileptic mode or normally. If they joined the pacemaker cells in burst (epileptic) firing, seizure propagation occurred, and normal cells outwith the Group II pool became involved and secondarily generalized seizures occurred. The state of arousal of both Group II cells and the normal cells surrounding the Group II pool was a significant modifying factor in whether seizure propagation occurred, supporting clinical observations that a person's mental state and level of arousal can influence seizure frequency both positively and negatively.

Epileptic activity not only produces synaptic, transmitter and receptor changes in the area of brain which generates it, but also in the areas of brain which receive the volleys of synchronous activity. In animals this produces 'secondary epileptogenesis' (*kindling*): this possibly happens in the human brain as well, producing a kind of 'electrical metastasis' and is an argument for suppressing, as quickly as possible, seizure activity (spontaneous seizures are a rare, but known, consequence of electroconvulsive therapy). It may be an explanation for the multifocal seizures seen so commonly in the learning disabled.

The effect of epileptic activity on transmitter and receptor function, both locally and remotely, may produce a variety of behavioural and cognitive changes that may be more damaging than the epilepsy itself. Those of you working in learning disability who need a good review of this whole area plus the allied knowledge of brain development are advised to read *Brain Development and Epilepsy*.[3]

Further reading

Alarcon G (1996) Electrophysiological aspects of interictal and ictal activity in human partial epilepsy. *Seizure* **5**:7–33.

Fisher R (1995) Cellular mechanisms of the epilepsies. In: *Epilepsy* (eds A Hopkins, S Shorvon and F Cascino). London: Chapman & Hall, pp. 39–58.

Jefferys J (1990) Basic mechanisms of focal epilepsies. *Ann Rev Neurosci* **1**: 395–415.

Neobels J (1992) Molecular genetics and epilepsy. In: *Recent Advances in Epilepsy* (eds TA Pedley and B Meldrum). London: Churchill Livingstone, pp. 1–13.

Satula T, Cascino G, Cavazos J et al (1989) Mossy fiber synaptic reorganisation in the epileptic temporal lobe. *Ann Neurol* **26**: 321–30.

Sisodiya S (1995) Wiring, dysmorphogenesis and epilepsy: a hypothesis. *Seizure* **4**: 169–185.

Epilepsy: aetiology

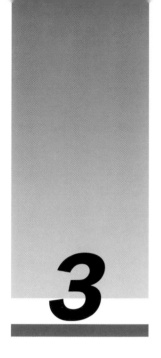

3

Epileptic activity is probably not always abnormal (although it seems to carry very little advantage for human kind). In a few animal species spontaneously occurring or reflex epilepsy is common, is maintained in the gene pool and must therefore have some biological advantage. Traces of this animal past still exist in the human brain which explains why, in some people, primary epileptogenesis seems to occur, presumably because of a genetically determined susceptibility (e.g. juvenile myoclonic epilepsy). If a sufficiently strong stimulus is applied to any human brain there will be a convulsive response (the basis of electroconvulsive therapy). In about 5% of the human population seizures occur apparently spontaneously or are triggered off by a stimulus to which most brains are inert. Such people are said to have a *low convulsive threshold.* Although convulsive threshold is genetically determined (and is lowest in infancy, childhood and adolescence) it is also lowered by breaches in the integrity of brain function caused by acquired or innate brain damage, metabolic or physiological changes in brain function or by some drugs. There is also an interaction between stress and convulsive threshold, not unsurprisingly in view of the intimate relationship between the GABA and benzodiazepine receptors.

Any condition which can lower convulsive threshold (by an effect on the ionic and transmitter mechanisms already described), either locally or generally, can cause epileptic seizures, although the actual cause of most epilepsies is as yet unknown and in at least 60% of people with established epilepsy the cause cannot be determined (see Table 3). Developing investigational techniques, particularly MRI, are beginning to teach us

about the causes of epilepsy in those cases whose aetiology is currently unknown, for example, *neuronal migration defects.* Functional scanning of the intact human brain (MR spectroscopy, positron emission tomography (PET)) will add to our knowledge of the causes of epilepsy.

It is likely that eventually we will understand the cause of most human epilepsies, particularly when we have investigative techniques that will enable us to understand the genetic chemistry of brain areas as well as their struc-

Table 3
Possible aetiology of epileptic seizures.

1. Genetic causes
   a) Metabolic disorders (e.g. phenylketonuria, Neimann–Pick disease)[6]
   b) 'Structural', e.g. tuberous sclerosis **(Figure 2)** neurofibromatosis
   c) Some primary generalized epilepsies (possibly polygenetic)
   d) Mitochondrial disorders
2. Developmental disorders e.g. neuronal migration disorder **(see Table 4)**
3. Intrauterine and perinatal injury[6] (anoxia) including febrile convulsions
4. Infection (e.g. encephalitis)
5. Trauma
6. Vascular
7. Tumour
8. Dementia and neurodegenerative disorder
9. Metabolic (e.g. hypoglycaemia)
10. Toxic (e.g. alcohol)

ture. It has been recognized that changes in gene expression will occur when epilepsy becomes established in brain tissue. Some genes have been shown to be switched on by seizure activity.[4] Genetic research in epilepsy is accelerating and will, comparatively soon, lead to new drug developments and rational drug therapy, rather than today's 'hit and miss' methods.[5]

Where a cause for epilepsy can be recognized, different causes appear at different ages. Some epilepsies are due to developmental disorders which mostly appear in infancy, as do genetic disorders **(see Table 4).** Perinatal hypoxia, developmental defects and inborn errors of metabolism are major causes of seizures in infants.[3,6] Some of these causes persist into, or present for the first time in, childhood.

Infections such as encephalitis or meningitis are relatively common causes of epilepsy in childhood: trauma results in epilepsy, particularly in young adults: cerebrovascular disease is the commonest identifiable cause of epilepsy among people over 50. Malignant cerebral tumours are relatively uncommon causes of epilepsy at all ages. Indolent or benign tumours, however, are a more common cause of focal epilepsies and are often not recognized for a long time after the onset of the epilepsy.

Table 4
Developmental disorders.

1.	*Dermoid/epidermoid cysts*
2.	*Cavernous haemangiomas* **(see Figure 3)**
3.	*Arteriovenous malformations* **(see Figure 4)**
4.	*Neuronal migration defects*
	a) Schizencephaly **(see Figure 5)**
	b) Hemimegalencephaly
	c) Lissencephaly
	d) Pachygyria
	e) Polymicrogyria
	f) Nodular heterotopias **(see Figure 6)**
5.	*Dysembryoplastic neuroepithelial tumour DNT* **(see Figure 7)**
6.	*Agenesis of the corpus callosum*

Febrile convulsions in early childhood, particularly if the convulsion is prolonged and the child becomes anoxic, are known to be associated with (usually unilateral) anoxic lesions in the hippocampus (hippocampal sclerosis or *mesial temporal sclerosis*) which later become the focus of medically intractable partial seizures (although often treatable with surgery). Mesial temporal sclerosis can now be recognized on MRI scanning. Some febrile convulsions are, however, expressions of a pre-existing neuronal defect. It is thought that not all mesial temporal sclerosis is caused by febrile convulsions.

Epilepsy, whether it is structurally or genetically determined, will often start at a time of stress in the patient's life, even though the cause has been present previously. Significant life events and stress will also cause exacerbations of seizure frequency.[7]

Genetic causes (**Table 3**) are important causes of epilepsy in childhood and in children with a developmental disorder.[3,6] Most present in infancy or early childhood but a few, particularly the progressive myoclonic epilepsies, may present later in life. Included in the genetic causes of progressive myoclonic epilepsies are the increasingly important mitochondrial disorders. Progressive myoclonic epilepsies may be particularly seen in learning disability populations as may the structural, usually dominantly inherited,

lesions such as tuberous sclerosis and neurofibromatosis. Some of the primary generalized epilepsies (for example juvenile myoclonic epilepsy) are almost certainly genetically determined although the chromosome responsible is still disputed: it is possible that it is a polygenetic disorder.[8]

Tuberous sclerosis (TS)

This is a dominantly inherited condition (sometimes with incomplete penetrance) which occurs in 1 in 7000 newborn children. At least two gene sites have been described. Most cases appear to be new mutations although careful screening of the family is essential when the condition is first recognized (including thorough examination of the skin under ultraviolet light, CT examination of the brain and ultrasound examination of the liver and kidneys). The condition is commonly, but not invariably, associated with learning difficulty (approximately 40%) and epilepsy (approximately 65%). It is said that learning disabilities do not occur in TS in the absence of seizures. The onset of seizures in an infant with TS is usually associated with rapid loss of intellect. It is possible to have the condition on its own, without epilepsy or learning difficulty, or to have it with epilepsy but not with learning difficulty. Behavioural difficulties are also common amongst people with tuberous sclerosis but are not always associated with seizures. Over half the children with both learning difficulty and tuberous sclerosis display autistic features: some may be hyperactive or have an attention deficit disorder. Behaviour disturbance is often much more of a problem than the seizures.

There are two classical signs of tuberous sclerosis, facial angiofibromas and multiple calcified subependymal glial nodules (**Figure 2**) but it has other distinguishing features (**see Table 5**). The typical skin lesions are illustrated in an excellent booklet published by the Tuberous Sclerosis Association.[9]

Skin lesions are common and can be diagnostic: facial angiofibromas (previously called adenoma sebaceum — this term is misleading and should be avoided) rarely occur before the age of 2 years (and may not appear until late adolescence or even later). They first appear as small red lesions. About 85% of people with tuberous sclerosis have them and they usually occur with a characteristic butterfly distribution, particularly involving the nasal folds: often profuse, they may be isolated and difficult to see.

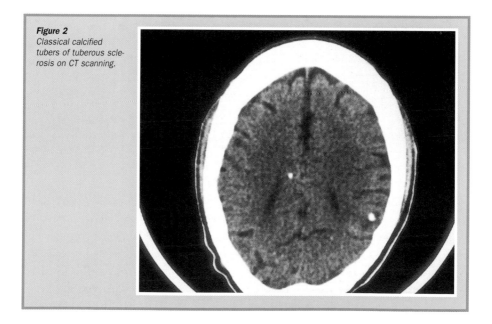

Figure 2
Classical calcified tubers of tuberous sclerosis on CT scanning.

Table 5
Diagnostic features of tuberous sclerosis.[10]

Primary diagnostic criteria	Secondary diagnostic criteria (two or more needed for diagnosis)
Facial angiofibromas	*Typical hypomelanic macules*
Ungual fibromas	*Bilateral polycystic kidneys*
Calcified retinal hamartomas	*Radiographic honeycomb lung (due to pulmonary lymphangiomyomatosis)*
Multiple cortical tubers (Figure 2)	
Multiple subependymal glial nodules	*Single cardiac rhabdomyoma*
	Single renal angiomyolipoma
Diagnostic criteria with an affected first degree relative	*Multiple subcortical hypomyelinated lesions or wedge shaped cortical-subcortical calcification*
Histologically proven giant cell astrocytoma	
Histologically proven cardiac rhabdomyomas or echocardiographic evidence of more than one lesion in children	
Single cortical tuber	
Single retinal hamartoma	
Possible additional primary diagnostic criteria	
Multiple bilateral renal angiomyolipomas	
Forehead fibrous plaque	
Shagreen patch	

'Ash leaf' lesions (hypomelanotic macules) occur in 80% of people with tuberous sclerosis: they are areas of depigmented skin that often lie in the line of a dermatome and are best seen under ultraviolet light. They can rarely occur in people who do not have TS.

Hyperpigmented macules (*cafe au lait* spots) are not pathognomonic of tuberous sclerosis, although commonly said to be. Forehead fibrous plaques (smooth, reddish, waxy-looking lesions) often occur very early in life and are characteristic of TS when present.

Shagreen patches are also characteristic of TS but only occur in 40% of people with it. They are a large area of thick and discoloured skin, usually on the back to one side of the midline. Fibromas also occur, particularly under the nails of both hands and feet and may cause characteristic grooving in the nail. Fibromas may occur around the gums: pitting of the teeth is common.

In about 50% of people with TS phakomas (hamartomas) can be seen in the retina. They are not all that easy to detect, unless they calcify, but are characteristic if they can be recognized. In the brain characteristic calcified tubers appear in the wall of the lateral ventricle (so called candle guttering) but can occur elsewhere in the cortex. They are best seen on CT scanning, but can be detected on MRI scanning using T2 weighted images (they appear as hyperintense signals). Giant cell astrocytomas also occur in the brain, and often give rise to hydrocephalus. Symptoms of vomiting and ataxia in young adults with learning difficulty and tuberous sclerosis should be investigated: these tumours usually enhance on MRI scanning with gadolinium.

Lesions may also be found in the heart (rhabdomyomas, which often decrease in size as the person grows older) in the kidney (angiomyolipomas and cysts) and are also to be found in the liver; cystic changes in the bones can also occur. Cystic disease of the lung is possible as are rectal polyps.

The diagnosis is made using primary diagnostic criteria (**see Table 5**) but this may not always be easy without cerebral CT scanning (although, as with Huntington's chorea, detecting a genetic marker may well eventually be the crucial test).

Other developmental disorders

Note. All these disorders usually require MRI scanning for their detection.

1. *Dermoid* and *epidermoid* cysts are hollow non-progressive cysts, sometimes with calcification in them; they may be resectable.

2. *Cavernous haemangiomas* (**Figure 3**) are small cyst like, often calcified, malformations of the walls of small blood vessels in the brain. They may rupture and can often be resected. They are a common cause of epilepsy.

3. *Arteriovenous malformations* (AVMs) (**Figure 4**) may be small or large and are complex maldevelopments of the junction

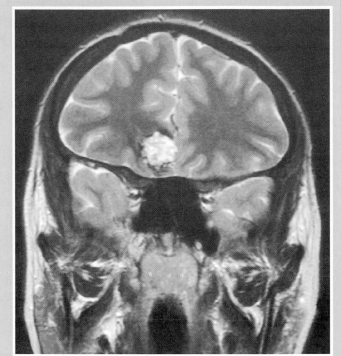

Figure 3
MRI of a cavernous haemangioma in the frontal area of a woman with intractable complex partial seizures. It was successfully removed with resulting seizure freedom. This lesion could not be seen on CT scanning.

between arteries and venous drainage. They can occur anywhere in the brain and may cause epilepsy by pressure effects, ischaemic 'steal' effects or after partial or complete rupture. There is a 3% cumulative annual risk of rupture, with resultant haemorrhage, so if they are recognized a neurosurgeon should be consulted.

4. *Neuronal migration defects* arise during intrauterine development of the brain.[11] In the developing brain neurons form in the midline and 'migrate' to the outer cortical mantle to eventually lie in orderly rows, which become interconnected. The neurons migrate down glial pathways; once arrived, about half are then pro-

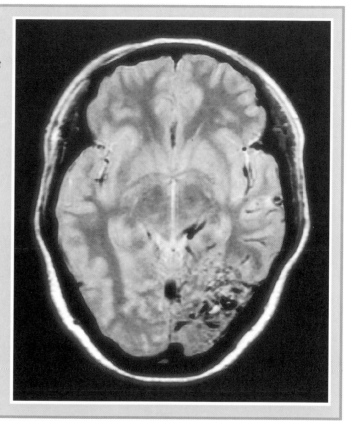

Figure 4
*MRI of a large arteriove-
nous malformation
(AVM) in a woman with
migraine and epilepsy; it
was not detected on CT
scanning.*

grammed to die (presumably more arrive
than are needed lest any miscarry on the
journey). The number programmed to
disappear depends to some extent on the
availability of post synaptic connections.
The cause of defects in neuronal migration may be genetic, may be due to infections (of the mother) or possibly may be
vascular.

Defects may relate to clumps of neurons
arriving in the wrong place (i.e. islands of

neurons in the white matter), neurons failing to arrive at all, to excessive loss of neurons or to failure to follow pro- grammed death. Clumps of heterotopic neurons, because of lack of external synap- tic control, are particularly likely to become foci for epileptic activity, as MRI scanning has revealed. It is likely, however, that the abnormal area of epileptogenic cortex is not limited to the observable MRI lesion so that resection may not lead to control of the epilepsy. Neuronal migration defects are often associated with learning difficulties and intractable epilep- sies, including infantile spasms and the Lennox–Gastaut syndrome. There are sev- eral distinct types, which may arise at dif- ferent stages of development.

- *Schizencephaly* (see **Figure 5**): cortex in the sylvian region is replaced by a grey matter lined cleft, often extending to the lateral ventricle. This may be unilateral or bilateral; if bilateral severe learning difficulty is likely, if unilateral, neuro- logical impairment may be slight and intelligence normal. Other neuronal migration defects may be present.

- *Hemimegalencephaly* is characterized by learning difficulty, hemiplegia, severe epilepsy starting in infancy and abnormal enlargement of one cerebral hemisphere, often containing polymicrogyria. It is believed to be due to failure of pro- grammed cell death.

- *Lissencephaly* is the result of faulty neuronal migration with missing or misshapen gyria (agyria, macrogyria). Cortex that contains neurons does not have the usual number of layers. It is associated with severe learning difficulty and intractable epilepsy. It is known to have a genetic basis.

5. *Pachygyria* is an area of cortex (as opposed to the whole cortex, as in lissencephaly) where neurons have not migrated prop- erly, leading to disruption or disappear- ance of the usual laminar layers of neurons.

- *Polymicrogyria* is accompanied by more cerebral convolutions than usual and an increased density of often haphazardly arranged neurons; it is often patchy. It may be associated with learning difficulty and other neuronal migration defects.

- *Nodular heterotopias* are discrete masses of neuronal aggregates found in the white matter, often near the lateral ventricles and sometimes associated with agenesis of the corpus callosum; a variant is laminar heterotopia (double cortex –

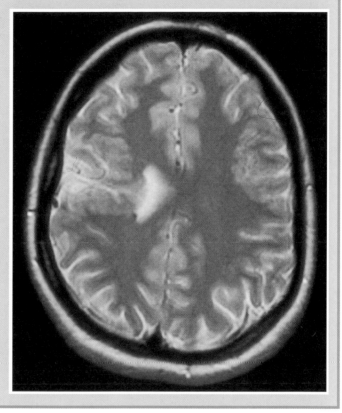

Figure 5
MRI of schizencephaly in a woman of normal intelligence with partial onset motor seizures. The lesion was invisible on CT scanning.

two distinct layers of cortex separated by white matter). Both may be associated with learning difficulty and intractable epilepsy. Periventricular nodular heterotopias **(Figure 6)** resemble those of tuberous sclerosis but do not calcify, are not associated with skin lesions and occur in females only.

Heterotopias may also be diffuse (and not recognizable by MRI) and only discovered in surgical specimens after temporal lobec-

Figure 6
Two views of MRI of
nodular heterotopia in a
patient with intractable
complex partial
seizures. CT scan
reported as normal.
Seizures resolved com-
pletely with gabapentin.
Note the nodules indent-
ing the walls of the lat-
eral ventricles: they are
not calcified.

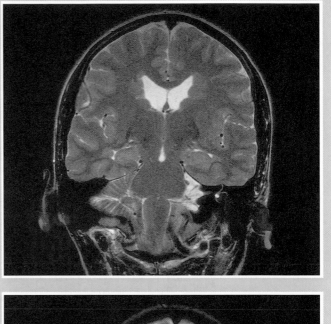

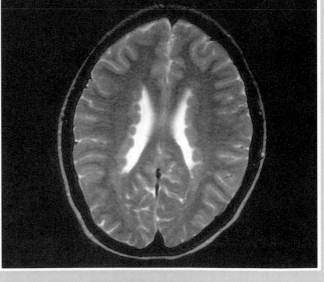

tomy. Meencke suggested that widespread microscopic microdysgensis is a cause of generalized seizures.[12]

6. *Dysembryoplastic neuroepithelial tumour* (DNT) **(Figure 7)** was only recently recognized, but is now known to be a common cause of intractable focal epilepsy. Although benign, on imaging it often looks malignant; it is a dysplastic calcified tumour, often resectable (with benefit to the epilepsy).

7. *Agenesis of the corpus callosum* is common in syndromes of learning difficulty and epilepsy including chromosomal disorders, genetic disorders, neuronal migration disorders, etc. Occasionally a missing

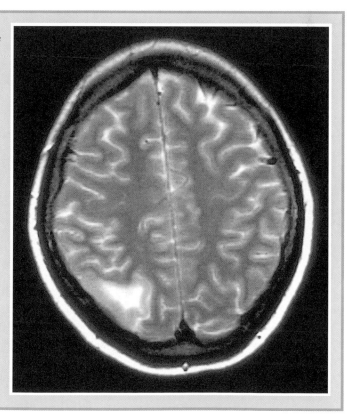

Figure 7
MRI of dysembryoplastic neuroepithelial tumour in a patient with intractable partial seizures and normal CT scan. The patient declined surgery.

corpus callosum can arise as an isolated defect, the epilepsy in that case being due to reduced inhibitory activity, due to loss of interhemispheric connections (although, interestingly, sectioning the corpus callosum in people with an intact corpus callosum but intractable seizures can result in control of seizures).

Intrauterine and perinatal anoxia and other injuries

These are known causes of epilepsy, which may be associated with learning difficulty.[6] Sometimes severe intrauterine vascular injury can occur to the brain, particularly embolic occlusion of a major artery, which is not recognized until epilepsy starts many years later, then on MRI scanning, an arachnoid or porencephalic cyst is found **(see Figure 8)**.

Infection

Infections (particularly in childhood) are a common cause of epilepsy. Encephalitis or meningitis is followed by epilepsy in a proportion of cases, particularly in patients with persistent neurological deficits or who have seizures during the acute stage of the illness. Herpes simplex encephalitis is commonly followed by epilepsy, often of a focal nature, even if the patient did not have seizures dur-

ing the acute stage. Post infective epilepsies are often difficult to control because they may be multifocal.

In other parts of the world, tuberculous meningitis and tuberculous granulomas of the brain and parasitic infections such as cysticercosis are extremely common causes of epilepsy. In this context it is important to remember that AIDS may present with epileptic seizures or with a mixed neurological and psychiatric presentation. The new form of Creutzfeldt Jakob disease (in which myoclonic jerks may be a feature even though the characteristic EEG pattern is absent) may present initially to the psychiatrist. In the learning disability world, patients may present with severe brain damage and intractable epilepsy after an encephalopathy supposedly related to immunization (usually with pertussis vaccine). There is probably a very small risk of this occurring after immunization but it *is* very small. Children are more at risk of epilepsy from the diseases which immunization controls, than from immunization itself.

Trauma is a cause of epilepsy but is only likely to occur if the brain injury associated with the trauma is severe (like a depressed fracture or penetration of the brain) or after a long post traumatic amnesia or if seizures occur in the first week after injury. Even so,

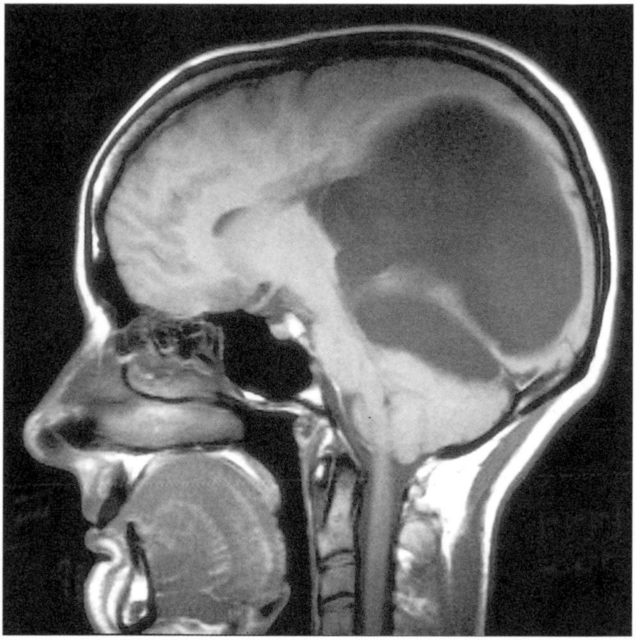

Figure 8
MRI of huge left hemi-sphere arachnoid cyst in a patient with minor motor seizures and nor-mal intellectual and physical development.

the chances of epilepsy after head injury are to some extent dependent on the patient's previous seizure threshold. It is a common observation (although little described in the literature) that patients with existing epilepsy, if they have a head injury with mild concussion, will have an increased frequency of seizures for some weeks afterwards. Some people, with no previous history of epilepsy,

after a minor head injury with a little concussion start having epileptic seizures shortly afterwards. It is difficult to say whether this minor head injury is responsible for the epilepsy or not. Often it must be no more that a coincidence, or the injury was the result of the person's first seizure, which went unrecognized. However minor head injury may occasionally be a cause of epilepsy.[13]

Vascular diseases

Apart from the vascular disorders already mentioned under developmental disorders, acute cortical infarction or haemorrhage (stroke) is also associated with epilepsy, particularly in the older population. Acute cortical stroke is accompanied, or shortly followed, by epilepsy in about 5–10% of cases. Epilepsy is also a late consequence of ischaemic lesions in the brain and is more likely to follow even small lacunar infarcts, although these are usually indicative of more widespread cerebrovascular disease. Epilepsy, particularly in middle or late life, may be *followed* by a stroke. This may, rarely, be because an unsuspected pre-existing vascular malformation was responsible for both, or merely be indicative of widespread cerebrovascular disease of which both the epilepsy and the stroke are a symptom. It is important not to diagnose Todd's paralysis, occurring after a motor seizure, as a stroke.

Tumours

Most doctors and many patients fear the onset of epilepsy in adult life means the development of a malignant brain tumour, but even in older age groups this is uncommon. In a recent community study in the UK tumours accounted for only 6% of newly diagnosed epilepsy (**Table 6**).[14] Rapidly growing malignant tumours, even if they present with epilepsy, usually are accompanied by other obvious symptoms of raised intracranial pressure, such as headache, vomiting and focal neurological signs and are not usually missed. Most tumours that are associated with epilepsy are either benign or indolent (although indolent tumours sometimes suddenly accelerate in growth, or suddenly expand because of haemorrhage into the tumour itself). Most tumours will present with a focal epilepsy related to the part of the brain in which they originate, but frontal tumours are associated with apparently gener-

Table 6
Causes of epilepsy in a community study of first seizures.[14]

Trauma	3%
Vascular	15%
Tumours	6%
Infections	2%
Degenerative	6%
Alcohol	7%
Cryptogenic/idiopathic	61%

Epilepsy: aetiology   **25**

alized tonic clonic seizures. Developments in scanning techniques, particularly high quality MRI, have revealed indolent or benign tumours not previously recognizable (e.g. DNT).

Dementia and neurodegenerative disorders

About 10% of patients with Alzheimer's disease also have epileptic seizures, usually of a partial nature, often not recognized. Up to 10% of patients with cerebrovascular dementia also have seizures, often intractable; sometimes the epilepsy presents first and the underlying dementia is not recognized or the patient's short-term memory deficits are ascribed to the epilepsy.

Metabolic disorders

These are an important cause of epilepsy in infants and children. Although outside the scope of this publication, any doctor working with a young learning difficulty population is advised to have a thorough understanding of the various types, and to seek the advice of a paediatric neurologist and paediatric biochemist if at all in doubt that one of his patients has such a disorder.[6,15] Metabolic causes of seizures in adolescents and adults are uncommon, but are occasionally seen in renal failure, hypoglycaemia, hypocalcaemia and hypercalcaemia. They may be the consequence of chronic water intoxication with resultant hyponatraemia (a not uncommon phenomenon in the chronically psychotic).

Toxins

Epilepsy may rarely be the result of intoxication with lead and other heavy metals; the most common toxins, however, are alcohol and drugs. Acute intoxication with alcohol can cause seizures as can acute withdrawal of alcohol in people who are habituated to it (tonic clonic seizures occur in 50% of patients with delirium tremens). People with chronic alcoholism can sometimes develop epileptic seizures, independent of intoxication or withdrawal, presumably as the result of brain damage caused by alcohol or because of brain injury sustained in falls. Complex vitamin and mineral deficiencies and overhydration may also play a part in the epilepsies associated with alcohol. Except in obvious intoxication or withdrawal seizures it is good clinical practice to investigate epilepsy, occurring in someone with a history of alcoholism, as carefully as one would with any other patient and not just ascribe it to 'rum fits'. Social drinking has no effect on seizure frequency and should not be discouraged. Many waking seizures ascribed to alcoholic indulgence the night before are, in fact, due to associated sleep deprivation and not the alcohol.

Drugs, particularly psychotropic drugs, can precipitate epileptic seizures in those already predisposed to the condition (particularly antidepressants and neuroleptics). It should not be assumed, however, that a patient who starts to have epileptic seizures shortly after the exhibition of an antidepressant or a neuroleptic necessarily has a drug induced epilepsy until full investigation. Patients with chronic epilepsy taking anticonvulsants in therapeutic doses may develop an increase in seizure frequency as a result of taking psychotropic medication. This response is unpredictable: a temporary worsening of seizure frequency may be a small price to pay for the relief of a severe depressive illness or a psychosis.

Further reading

Schacter S (1995) The neurobiology of epilepsy: Developmental biology and clinical aspects. In: *Epilepsy* (eds A Hopkins, S Shorvon and F Cascino). London: Chapman & Hall. pp. 25–34.

Schwartzkroin P, Moshe S, Noebels J and Swann J (eds) (1995) *Brain Development and Epilepsy*. New York: Oxford University Press.

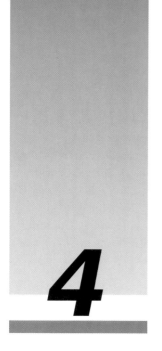

Epidemiology of epilepsy

The literature on the epidemiology of epilepsy is a mess and a muddle, because data are based on the study of different populations, with different definitions of epilepsy (e.g. when epilepsy has ceased to be epilepsy, or whether a first seizure is counted as epilepsy) and because of different methods of ascertainment. Doctors have long been taught that epilepsy is predominantly a disease of childhood which occasionally escapes into adult life. Modern epidemiological studies have shown that this is not true: the onset of epilepsy is almost as common in middle and late age as it is in childhood and the prevalence of epilepsy rises with age. For a careful review of this contentious area see Hopkins and Shorvon.[16]

A recent UK epidemiological study suggests that the prevalence of epilepsy is between 0.5 and 1 person per hundred.[17] Other studies have shown that the cumulative incidence of first unprovoked seizures by the age of 75 may be nearly 5% and the cumulative incidence for epilepsy itself is about 3%.[18] Most people who have a first unprovoked epileptic seizure will eventually have another (but, as we shall see later, it can be very difficult to determine if a first seizure is an epileptic one or not), and many first seizures are provoked.

Epilepsy, usually, has a good prognosis: about 30% of all cases only have a few seizures before the attacks stop: in this group epilepsy may well be self-limiting and not need treatment. In 30% of cases seizures are usually controlled with an anti-epileptic drug and spontaneous remission may occur, with only a small chance of recurrence if medication is withdrawn. About 20% of seizures can be controlled with medication but it cannot be withdrawn (because the relapse rate is high). Recurrent episodes of relapse are not uncommon, even with continued medication (personality, social and stress factors may play a part in relapse in this group). About 20% of patients with epilepsy have a poor prognosis and seizures continue despite treatment. These, of course, are often the patients encountered by the specialist in learning disability; the more the integrity of brain function is breached by damage or metabolic changes, the less likely seizures are to be controlled. By and large, the greater the degree of intellectual impairment in people with learning disability, the greater the chance of epilepsy.

The prognosis of epilepsy may be to some extent dependent on the speed with which it comes under control with medication: after two years of continuing seizures the prognosis for complete control of seizures is much poorer. Whether this is actually true, and 'seizures beget seizures', is still fiercely debated: see Sadzot[19] for a review. Patients with chronic epilepsy which has not come under control (who are the target for trials of new compounds for epilepsy) often, however, have a fluctuating course in the frequency of their seizures with short-term remissions and exacerbations (probably related to the natural history of epilepsy itself, but sometimes due to changes in stress levels and social wellbeing).

Epilepsy has a *morbidity rate* (burns, fractures, etc.) which has not been adequately defined in the general population. It is likely to be higher in those with severe intractable epilepsy and living in institutions or community care. Most of the handicaps of epilepsy (apart from the epilepsies with associated brain disease) are psychological and social and will be described in a later section.

Epilepsy also has a *mortality rate*, partly from the cause of the seizure (as in stroke or cerebral tumour), partly as the result of accidents sustained during a seizure (e.g. falling down the stairs or drowning — drowning in the domestic bath is the commonest accidental cause of death in people with epilepsy: children with epilepsy are seven times more likely to drown, or nearly drown, than other children, when swimming). Suicide is more commonly represented in people with epilepsy than in the general population (see the section on Depression and epilepsy). The commonest cause of death in epilepsy is so called 'sudden unexpected death in epilepsy' (SUDEP). This tends to occur in young people between the ages of 20 and 40 (especially males) who have convulsive or complex partial seizures. The patient is either found dead after a seizure or has a seizure, appears to recover and then is found dead later. Possibly one in two hundred people with chronic epilepsy die this way each calendar year. The cause of these deaths remains a matter of conjecture but recent research has suggested that it is a respiratory death which possibly explains why most cases occur at night when the patient is alone.[20]

Classification of epilepsy

5

Although, like its epidemiology, knowledge of the classification of epilepsy is imperfect, doctors should attempt, both
when communicating with each other and with their
patients, to use the international classification of seizures,
despite its imperfections **(see Table 7)**.

'Partial seizures are those in which, in general, the first clinical
electroencephalographic changes indicate initial activation of a
system of neurons limited to part of one cerebral hemisphere.
A partial seizure is classified primarily on the basis of whether
or not consciousness is impaired during the attack. When consciousness is not impaired, the seizure is classified as a *simple
partial seizure.* When consciousness is impaired the seizure is
classified as a *complex partial seizure.* Impaired consciousness is
defined as the inability to respond normally to exogenous
stimuli by virtue of altered awareness and/or responsiveness'.[21]

'Generalized seizures are those in which the first clinical
changes indicate initial involvement of both hemispheres.
Consciousness may be impaired and this impairment may be
the initial manifestation. Motor manifestations are bilateral.
The ictal electroencephalographic patterns initially are bilat-

Table 7
International League Against Epilepsy classification of epileptic seizures.[21]

A. Simple Partial Seizures (consciousness not impaired)

1. *With motor signs:*
   a) *Focal motor without march*
   b) *Focal motor with march (Jacksonian)*
   c) *Versive*
   d) *Postural*
   e) *Phonatory (vocalization or arrest of speech)*

2. *With somatosensory or special sensory symptoms (simple hallucinations, e.g.. tingling, light flashes, buzzing):*
   a) *Somatosensory*
   b) *Visual*
   c) *Auditory*
   d) *Olfactory*
   e) *Gustatory*
   f) *Vertiginous*

3. *With autonomic symptoms or signs (including epigastric sensation, pallor, sweating, flushing, piloerection and pupillary dilatation).*

4. *With psychic symptoms (disturbance of higher cerebral function). These symptoms rarely occur without impairment of consciousness and are much more commonly experienced as complex partial seizures.*
   a) *Dysphasic*
   b) *Dysmnesia (e.g. déjà vu)*
   c) *Cognitive (e.g. dreamy states and distortions of time sense)*
   d) *Affective (fear, anger, etc)*
   e) *Illusions (e.g. macropsia)*
   f) *Structural hallucinations (e.g. music, scenes)*

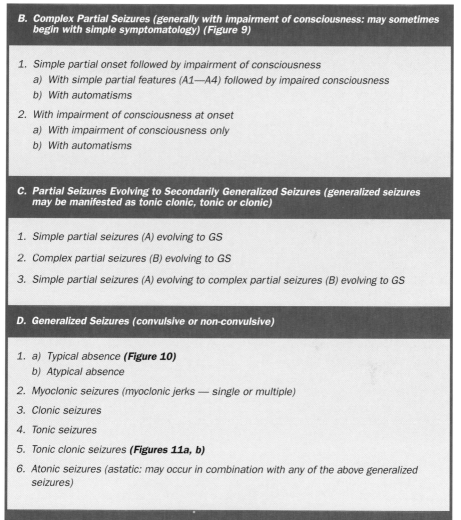

B. Complex Partial Seizures (generally with impairment of consciousness: may sometimes begin with simple symptomatology) (Figure 9)

1. Simple partial onset followed by impairment of consciousness
    a) With simple partial features (A1—A4) followed by impaired consciousness
    b) With automatisms
2. With impairment of consciousness at onset
    a) With impairment of consciousness only
    b) With automatisms

C. Partial Seizures Evolving to Secondarily Generalized Seizures (generalized seizures may be manifested as tonic clonic, tonic or clonic)

1. Simple partial seizures (A) evolving to GS
2. Complex partial seizures (B) evolving to GS
3. Simple partial seizures (A) evolving to complex partial seizures (B) evolving to GS

D. Generalized Seizures (convulsive or non-convulsive)

1. a) Typical absence **(Figure 10)**
    b) Atypical absence
2. Myoclonic seizures (myoclonic jerks — single or multiple)
3. Clonic seizures
4. Tonic seizures
5. Tonic clonic seizures **(Figures 11a, b)**
6. Atonic seizures (astatic: may occur in combination with any of the above generalized seizures)

E. Unclassified seizures

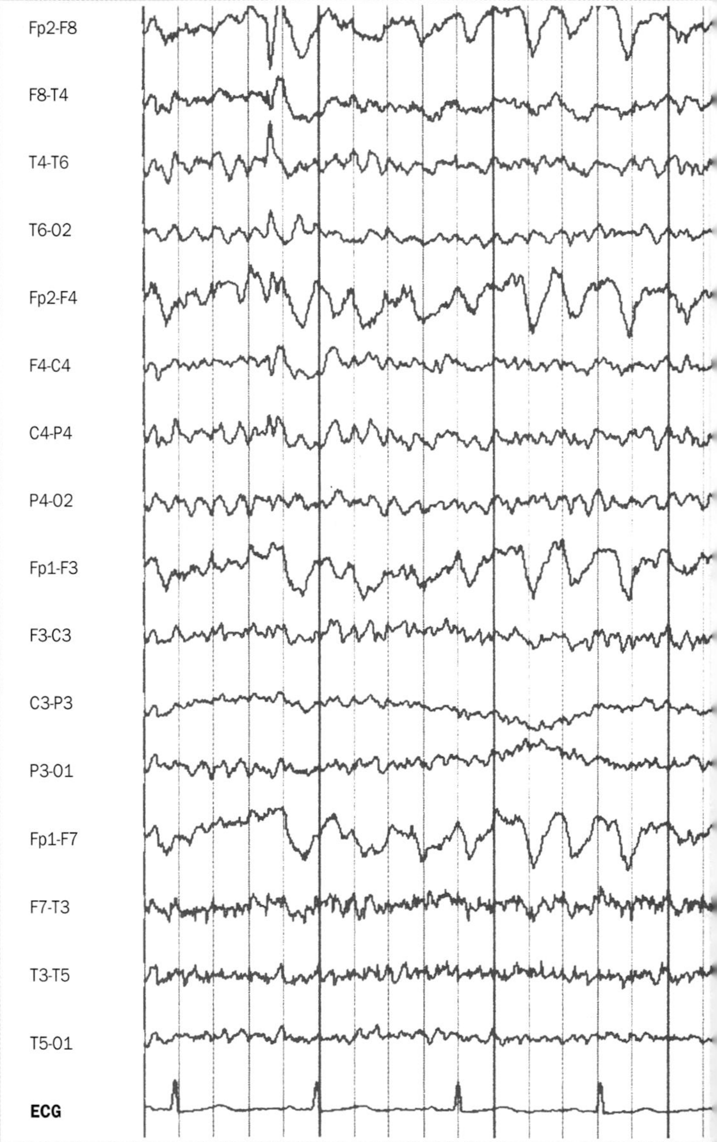

Figure 9
Focal EEG abnormality in patient with complex partial seizures. Right temporal lobe spikes.

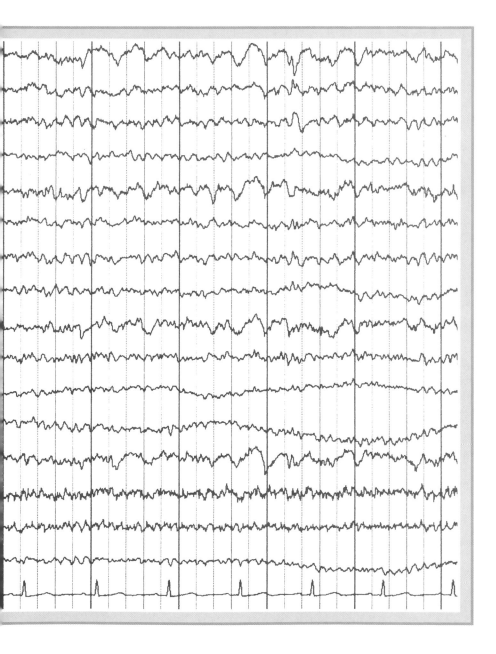

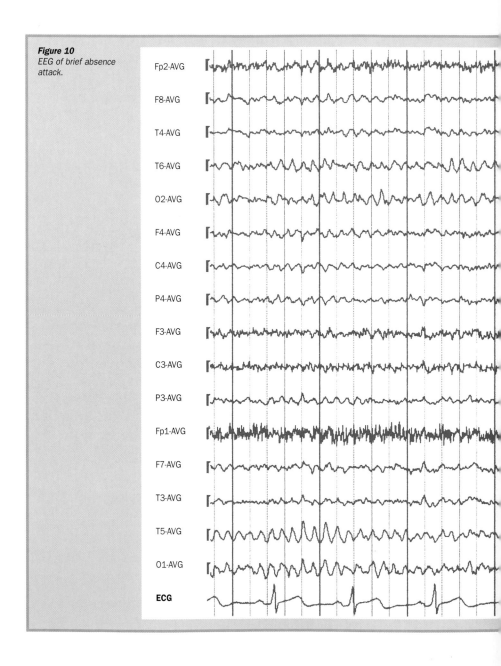

Figure 10
EEG of brief absence attack.

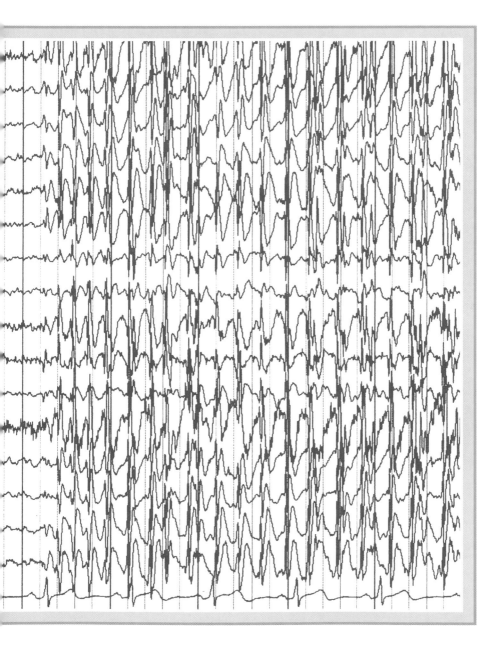

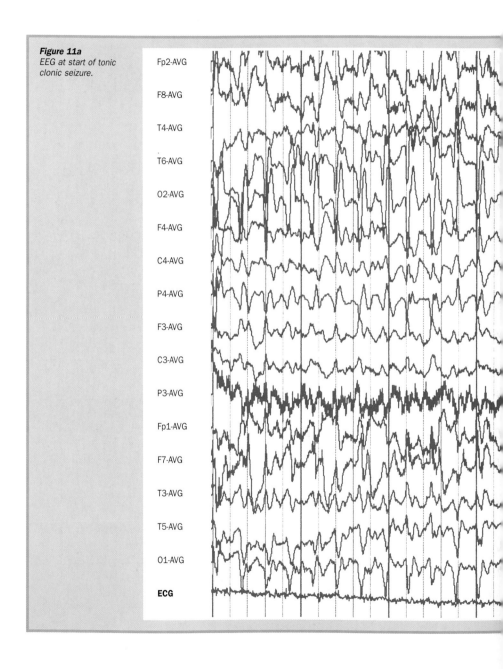

Figure 11a
EEG at start of tonic clonic seizure.

Fp2-AVG
F8-AVG
T4-AVG
T6-AVG
O2-AVG
F4-AVG
C4-AVG
P4-AVG
F3-AVG
C3-AVG
P3-AVG
Fp1-AVG
F7-AVG
T3-AVG
T5-AVG
O1-AVG
ECG

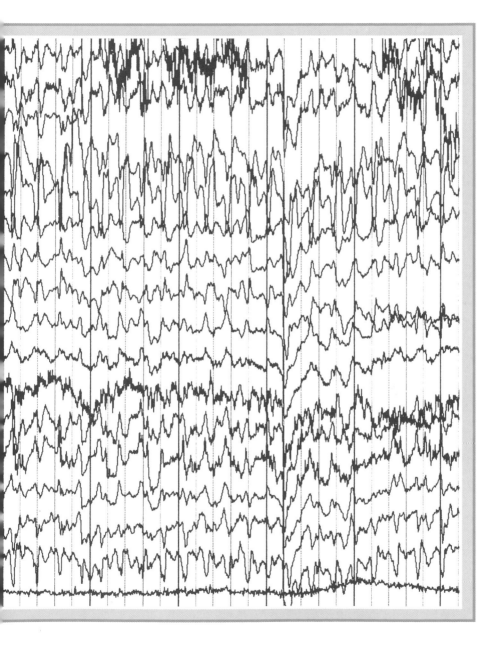

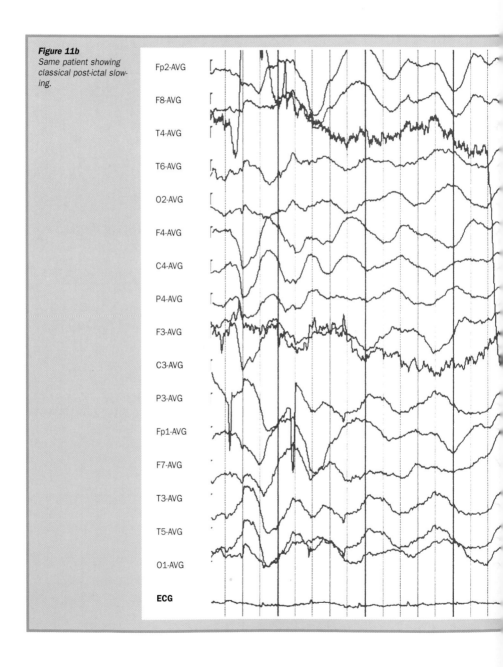

Figure 11b
Same patient showing classical post-ictal slowing.

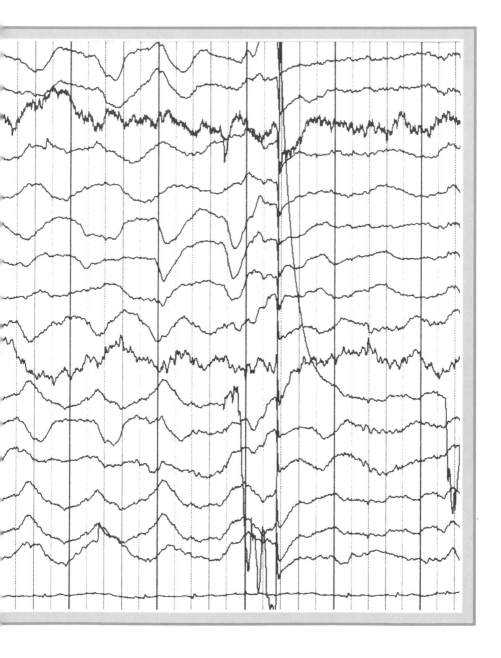

eral and presumably reflect neuronal discharge which is widespread in both hemispheres'.[21]

Common phenomena in frontal lobe seizures

The motor movements of a simple partial seizure may be tonic or clonic and are frequently adversive — a turning of the head and eyes to one side sometimes accompanied by stiffening or jerking of the arm on the same side (and, sometimes, the leg). An adversive seizure does not necessarily localize the epileptic discharge to the opposite frontal lobe as it may be caused by discharge in the ipsilateral frontal lobe or from the temporal lobe; primary generalized tonic clonic seizures during the tonic phase (or in tonic seizures themselves) may have a misleading adversive start.

Tonic or clonic motor seizures may start in, and involve the whole of, or part of, the arm or leg; sometimes jerking starts in the periphery of the limb and gradually recruits and spreads to involve the whole of it, although this classical 'Jacksonian march' is uncommon. Motor seizures may be followed by a transient weakness of the involved limb (Todd's paralysis). Tonic motor seizures involve posturing of a limb which may look 'functional'.

COMMON PHENOMENA IN TEMPORAL LOBE ONSET SEIZURES

Autonomic: *sweating, bradycardia, pallor, cardiac arrythmias (can be confused with vasovagal attacks)*

Psychic: *jamais vu, déjà vu, fear, ecstasy, depression, amnesia, derealization, depersonalization, rarely anger*

Sensory: *hallucinations/illusions of vision (formed), olfactory (usually unpleasant), auditory and gustatory*

Visceral: *nausea, 'rising' feeling in epigastrium*

Automatisms: *lip smacking, chewing, swallowing, searching, fumbling, wandering, scratching, resistive, undressing. Vocalization may occur; motionless stare*

Mesiobasal discharge: *autonomic, psychological and visceral phenomena*

Amygdala/uncal discharge: *olfactory/gustatory symptoms*

Superior temporal gyrus: *auditory hallucinations*

Lateral cortex: *visual hallucinations*

Bilateral spread: *automatisms, impairment of consciousness*

Unilateral seizure discharge in a frontal lobe may cause *bilateral*, sometimes apparently purposive, motor movements. Speech phenomena may occur — speech arrest, muttering, the speaking of recognizable, but out of context, phrases; they are not particularly helpful in accurately localizing where the seizure discharge is and do not imply that the seizure discharge must be on the left.

Sudden atonic seizures can occur. Frontal seizures are abrupt in onset, generalize rapidly and are usually brief, at night and cluster; status epilepticus may be the first presentation. Some frontal seizures (cingulate and prefrontal) resemble temporal lobe seizures and cannot be clinically distinguished from them.

Common phenomena of parietal seizures

Mainly sensory (focal tingling, numbness, tickling, 'electric shock', pain (which can be severe burning), sexual sensations (sexual *behaviours* are usually frontally based), paralysis, body image disturbance.

Common phenomena in occipital onset seizures

Unformed visual hallucinations (coloured spots or flashes of light), transient blindness, epileptic nystagmus, transient loss of colour vision.

Common phenomena in generalized seizures

Typical absences are brief impairments of consciousness (for which the victim has no awareness) accompanied by 'classic' generalized three per second spike wave EEG activity **(Figure 10)**. Atypical absences are not accompanied by this classical EEG pattern (but usually generalized irregular poly spike and wave) the victims usually know they have had one and there is often brief post ictal confusion. Typical absences may just involve a brief absence with no movement or brief clonic jerks of eyes, or head (rarely of limbs).

A brief absence usually accompanies other generalized seizures including myoclonic jerks, atonic and tonic seizures. Myoclonic jerks are brief, single or multiple, shock like jerks which may involve all the limbs or just the upper or lower limbs and may be unilateral and are usually, but not invariably, accompanied by loss of awareness. In atonic seizures there is sudden loss of muscle tone accompanied by falling: in tonic seizures there is a sudden stiffening followed by falling; there is usually a brief loss of awareness in both (so that patients cannot protect themselves). In tonic clonic seizures (the classical 'grand mal') there is a tonic phase of varying severity and duration — in which the patient falls and may bite the tongue, utters a characteristic cry and may be incontinent followed by clonic jerking and later recovery of consciousness.

Epilepsy can also be classified syndromically.[22] This is extremely important in children: syndromic classification is becoming more important in adolescents and adults with epilepsy. Recognizing a true epileptic syndrome gives far more information than making a purely localization related diagnosis as it can imply aetiology, prognosis and correct management. As the genetic chemistry of epilepsy is better understood syndromic classification will become more common. The proposed International League Against Epilepsy syndromic classification of epilepsy is contained in **Table 8**. Some of the important syndromes, particularly in learning disability practice, are described below.

West syndrome

This syndrome is characterized by spasms (flexor, extensor, clonic or myoclonic) occurring in the setting of developmental arrest and the characteristic EEG pattern of hypsarrhythmia. The syndrome always appears by one year and is commoner in boys. Most cases are symptomatic, related to perinatal asphyxia, cerebral malformations such as

tuberous sclerosis, pre- or postnatal infection or metabolic disorders. A few cases (20%) are cryptogenic. There is controversy about the best form of treatment but most UK experts now accept that vigabatrin given early is the most effective form of treatment and are cautious about the use of steroids.[6] Although the prognosis is often gloomy in some patients a marked degree of recovery is possible; most victims, however, remain with some epilepsy and some degree of learning difficulty, if not profoundly learning disabled.

Lennox–Gastaut syndrome

Although comparatively rare (about 1% of all new epilepsics) this is an important syndrome particularly in the learning disability field. Sometimes the West syndrome passes into the Lennox–Gastaut syndrome but most cases arise de novo usually appearing at between 1 and 8 years old. Characteristically there is a rapid onset of multiple seizure types (myoclonic jerks, atonic (drop) attacks, atypical absences and tonic and tonic clonic seizures). There is a characteristic EEG with a slow spike wave pattern. Ninety per cent of patients develop moderate to severe learning difficulties — sometimes the result of uncontrolled seizures. Seizures tend to be refractory

Table 8
ILAE Classification of Epilepsy Syndromes.[22]

A. Localization-related (focal, local, partial) epilepsies and syndromes.

1. Idiopathic (with age-related onset)
   a) Benign childhood epilepsy with centro-temporal spikes
   b) Childhood epilepsy with occipital paroxysms
   c) Primary reading epilepsy

2. Symptomatic
   a) Chronic progressive epilepsia partialis continua of childhood (Kojewnikow's syndrome)
   b) Syndromes characterized by seizures with specific modes of presentation.

3. Cryptogenic (presumed symptomatic but aetiology unknown)

B. Generalized epilepsies and syndromes

1. Idiopathic (with age-related onset, listed in order of age)
   a) Benign neonatal familial convulsions
   b) Benign neonatal convulsions
   c) Benign myoclonic epilepsy in infancy
   d) Childhood absence epilepsy
   e) Juvenile absence epilepsy
   f) Juvenile myoclonic epilepsy
   g) Epilepsy with grand mal (generalized tonic-clonic seizures) on awakening
   h) Other generalized idiopathic epilepsies not defined above
   i) Epilepsies with seizures precipitated by specific modes of activation (reflex and reading epilepsies)

2. Cryptogenic or symptomatic (in order of age)
   a) West's syndrome
   b) Lennox–Gastaut syndrome
   c) Epilepsy with myoclonic-astatic seizures
   d) Epilepsy with myoclonic absences

Cont'd.

3. Symptomatic
    a) Non-specific aetiology
       • Early myoclonic encephalopathy
       • Early infantile epileptic encephalopathy with suppression burst
       • Other symptomatic generalized epilepsies not defined above
    b) Specific syndromes/aetiologies
       • Cerebral malformations
       • Inborn errors of metabolism including pyridoxine dependency and disorders
         frequently presenting as progressive myoclonic epilepsy

C. Epilepsies and syndromes undetermined, whether focal or generalized

1. With both generalized and focal seizures
    a) Neonatal seizures
    b) Severe myoclonic epilepsy in infancy
    c) Epilepsy with continuous spike-waves during slow wave sleep
    d) Acquired epileptic aphasia (Landau-Kleffner syndrome)
    e) Other undetermined epilepsies not defined above
2. Without unequivocal generalized or focal features

D. Special syndromes

1. Situation-related seizures
    a) Febrile convulsions
    b) Isolated seizures or isolated status epilepticus
    c) Seizures occurring only when there is an acute metabolic or toxic
       event due to factors such as alcohol, drugs, eclampsia, non-ketotic
       hyperglycaemia

to standard anticonvulsants and the keto-genic diet is still used for this condition. Lamotrigine however appears to be at least moderately effective if used early and felba-mate, although potentially toxic, can also be tried. Topiramate is also worthy of a cautious trial. If a patient has severe atonic seizures that cannot be controlled in any other way, surgical section of the corpus callosum may be helpful.

Rasmussen's syndrome (sometimes called Kojewnikow's syndrome)

This is a chronic localized apparent encephalitis (although no virus has ever been isolated). It usually starts in childhood, with a slowly progressive neurological deficit (usu-ally hemiparesis) with gradual mental retarda-tion and intractable focal seizures, often with epilepsia partialis continua. It usually ends in severe intellectual and physical handicap, and may be fatal. It is probably more common than generally realized: hemispherectomy may help; the syndrome is resistant to anti-convulsants.

Landau–Kleffner syndrome

This disorder is characterized by, usually sud-den, intense loss of language followed by epileptic seizures which may be generalized or partial. Occasionally EEG examination before the onset of the seizures may show focal paroxysmal EEG activity. Seizures are usually controllable but the aphasia takes a long time to clear and only rarely completely recovers; subsequent behaviour disturbance (and occasionally severe learning difficulty) is common.

Juvenile myoclonic epilepsy

This is a syndrome of adolescents and younger adults which is common (perhaps 10% of clinic referrals) but is often unrecog-nized. Characteristically myoclonic jerks develop in the early morning in late child-hood followed by generalized tonic clonic seizures occurring within the first hour of waking and sometimes absences; many patients are also photosensitive. Myoclonic jerks are made worse by carbamazepine and vigabatrin and the syndrome is often not rec-ognized for what it is because of a failure to recognize the characteristic myoclonic jerks and the seizures' characteristic relationship to waking. Stress, relative sleep deprivation and possibly excess alcohol intake may precipitate seizures (not the happiest news for the adolescent!).

The importance of this syndrome is that although seizures can usually be controlled with valproate or lamotrigine they will usually return, no matter how long they have been controlled, if drugs are withdrawn; it also has a genetic element. The gene for this syndrome is believed to lie on chromosome 6 although evidence is conflicting. Recognizing the syndrome enables a proper prognosis and correct treatment to be given.

Management of epilepsy

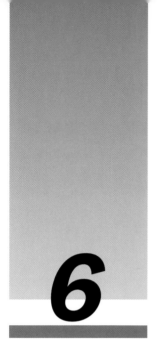

6

Management at onset

When faced with a patient who has begun to have an attack disorder (a sudden, paroxysmal, change in behaviour, thinking, feeling or cognition) there is a wide differential diagnosis which should be considered carefully (see separate section Is it epilepsy?). There is evidence that the diagnosis of epilepsy is often made too soon and on inadequate evidence and once made is difficult to change.[7] A proportion of people with chronic epilepsy actually have some other attack disorder which has been consistently mislabelled. It is worthwhile therefore trying to get the diagnosis right in the first place. The diagnosis of epilepsy may be difficult to make and may need time to elucidate; it should never be made hurriedly and should only be made when clinically certain.

Diagnosis is based on a careful history, both from the person who has the attacks and from a witness. It is important to record events that occurred before the attack and afterwards as well as what happened during it **(see Table 9)**. The witness' account may well be distorted by fear (a mother, for instance, who sees her child have its first seizure and thinks

Table 9
Seizure observation.

1. How did the patient feel before the event?
2. In what environment did the event take place?
3. What was the event like?
4. Was the patient standing, sitting or lying?
5. Time of day or night?
6. Did anything 'trigger' the event?
7. Was there a warning? (aura)
8. Could the person stop the event by bending down or any other manoeuvre?
9. Was there a fall?
10. Was the patient unconscious or aware (fully or vaguely)?
11. If unconscious, how long for?
12. What was the patient like while unconscious?
13. Was pulse/respiration recorded?
14. Was there incontinence/tongue biting/excess saliva?
15. Was there any associated injury/bruising?
16. What was the patient like after the attack?

that the child is dying is unlikely to be an objective witness of the event) and will also be affected by honest ignorance. An observation important to a doctor may not be thought so by a lay person or may be misinterpreted (characteristic, noisy, restarting of breathing after a tonic clonic seizure, for instance, may be described as 'gasping for breath' which may mislead the doctor into thinking that the witness is describing hyperventilation). It is often useful, when trying to obtain a history from witnesses, to show them videotaped examples of the kind of seizure they are trying to describe to see if the image matches their experience.

Although epilepsy remains a clinical diagnosis, based on the description given, certain aids to diagnosis are available. After what may have been a complex partial seizure or a tonic clonic seizure, a highly significant increase in serum prolactin level above baseline can be measured,[23] if blood is taken 20 minutes after the start of the seizure (this response exhausts quickly so cannot be used to confirm status epilepticus). It is important to measure a baseline level (at the same time of the day) when a seizure has not occurred to confirm this. It is possible now to record an EEG during a seizure, if there is diagnostic doubt (see later) or an ECG. With the advent of cheap portable video cameras and recorders, it is often possible for friends or family to videotape a seizure for later analysis by a doctor.

When a clinical diagnosis of an epileptic seizure has been made, decisions about investigation are needed. The amount of investigation necessary will depend on the kind of seizure the patient has had (partial seizures need more investigation than what are clearly primary generalized seizures) but epilepsy is often under investigated. The *Epilepsy Needs Document*[24] sets out what are considered to be the minimum standards of investigation for epilepsy in the UK.

Everyone who has clinically diagnosed epilepsy should have at least one EEG (many patients, perhaps 50%, will need at least two). Obviously the patient should have a thorough physical and neurological screen and a psychological/psychiatric screen as well (this is often not done). If there is clear evidence that the epilepsy may have a partial onset then MRI scanning is appropriate (infants should have a metabolic screen). Within the professional lifetime of most of the young doctors reading this a genetic screen will also become appropriate for all epilepsies.

Investigation is aimed at determining the cause of the epilepsy, in case appropriate action needs to be taken (e.g. surgery for a tumour), and is also aimed at localizing where in the brain the seizures are coming from (which helps in decisions about management) and in identifying syndromes and precipitants (e.g. photosensitivity).

Electroencephalographic investigation

An EEG is not a magic black box into which the patient is fed at one end and an answer comes out at the other. The EEG does *not* make the diagnosis of epilepsy: it merely helps to localize the origin of the epilepsy and helps to describe seizure types and, sometimes, provide syndromic diagnosis. A normal EEG does not mean that the patient does not have epilepsy (even, under certain circumstances, if a seizure is recorded whilst the EEG is in progress). Likewise interictal abnormalities in an EEG may support a diagnosis of epilepsy, but may not. Spike and wave activity, either focal or generalized, can, for instance, be found in some people who have never had an epileptic seizure in their lives. Until recently recording was made in real time on paper, but now modern EEG machines are digital and results can be read directly from a monitor screen and stored on disc. Examples of abnormalities related to epilepsy are given in Figures 9–13 taken from digital recordings. Cooperation with the skilled technicians responsible for the recording and the neurophysiologist responsible for its interpretation will lead to a more meaningful interpretation (**see Table 10**).

An EEG investigating epilepsy must include full photosensitivity testing (**Figure 12**) (see the section on Reflex epilepsy) and the patient must also be properly hyperventilated (as this will often induce abnormality not otherwise seen). Other provocative EEG techniques include sleep deprivation: a sleep deprived EEG should include a period of recording when the patient is awake but sleep deprived (having been awake all night) and a period of recording when the patient is drowsy before falling asleep and whilst asleep (about 20% of people with epilepsy only have seizures in their sleep so recording in sleep may provide information that is not available from an awake recording). Since some seizures occur at sleep onset and some occur at sleep offset a sufficient time asleep should be recorded if possible to allow nat-

ural waking; deep sleep is usually less informative, however. A sleep deprived EEG requires planning (and a quiet room); all night sleep deprivation will be needed to produce a seizure in sleep, but lesser degrees of sleep deprivation may help induce abnormality, particularly if recorded at times in the day when natural drowsiness is likely (e.g. after lunch).

Ictal EEG recording

The full investigation of epilepsy, using electrophysiology, demands recording an actual seizure. This is only a practical proposition if the patient is having a sufficient number of seizures for the apparatus to catch one (*at least three a week*) or a typical seizure can be provoked.

Ambulatory EEG monitoring

Up to 16 channels (more usually 8) of EEG can be recorded by electrodes carefully glued on the head connected to amplifiers worn on a collar: a recorder (a little like a 'Walkman') is worn on a belt. The device is socially acceptable and has the great virtue that it can record at work, at school and in the home where seizures tend to occur. Its disadvantages are that it is very prone to artefact (**Figure 13**) (which can be mistaken for epilepsy, e.g. chewing artefact), needs highly skilled interpretation and, although a con-

Table 10
Getting the best out of an EEG service: notes for the psychiatrist.

When requesting an EEG

1. Do remember that the EEG does not reveal cerebral tumours, measure personality or intelligence nor yet reveal states of mind or what the patient is thinking (i.e. do not ask silly questions!).

2. Do appreciate an EEG does not make or break the diagnosis of epilepsy (although it may confirm the diagnosis if a seizure is recorded). A normal EEG does not mean the patient does not have epilepsy.

3. It is an essential tool in the investigation of epilepsy but it needs help; its interpretation is easier if the neurophysiologist making the report has discussed the case with you, has been given a full history of the attacks under investigation (with any obvious precipitant) and knows what medication the patient is taking.

4. It would be a courtesy to the technicians in the department to be warned if a patient is potentially violent or self destructive or needs particularly tactful or careful handling (EEG equipment is expensive and good technicians hard to replace!). Always provide a suitable escort if the patient is at all likely to be difficult.

5. If possible avoid the prescription of benzodiazepine drugs for 14 days before the test; but if a patient is taking one of these drugs as an anticonvulsant or to control disruptive behaviour then do not withdraw it.

6. Be prepared to learn: do not just read the report but discuss it with the technicians or the neurophysiologist and look at the actual recording: both are interested in your patient and are keen to help you.

7. Don't ask for ambulatory or telemetered EEG recording unless the patient is having enough seizures or they can be provoked or anticipated. Discuss your requirements with the technicians in the department.

---

temporaneous video recording can be made of the patient, the recording is not usually time locked to the EEG signal. Because of the limited number of channels recorded, accurate localization of epileptic discharge is not possible: a normal ambulatory EEG record during a seizure may be misleading.

Telemetered EEG

This form of continual day and night EEG recording has to take place in hospital in an especially equipped room; although patients have some freedom of movement, their activity is restricted. A full set of electrodes

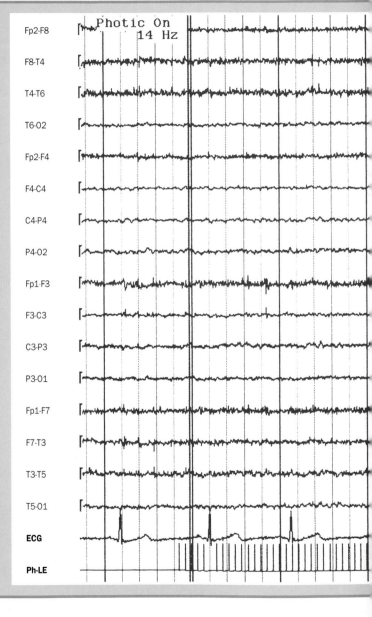

Figure 12a

Photosensitivity: EEG record. The patient was exposed to a flickering light (at 14 cycles per second) at a standard distance. There was a marked photoconvulsive response approximately 3 seconds after the onset of the light stimulus (marked at the bottom of the record as vertical lines). The patient also had primary generalized epilepsy.

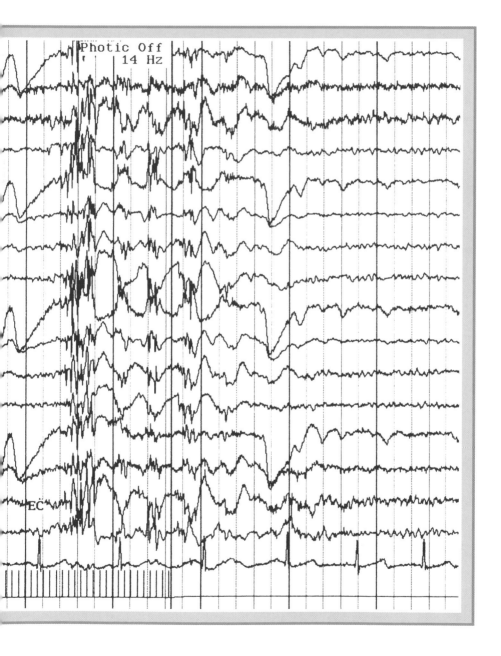

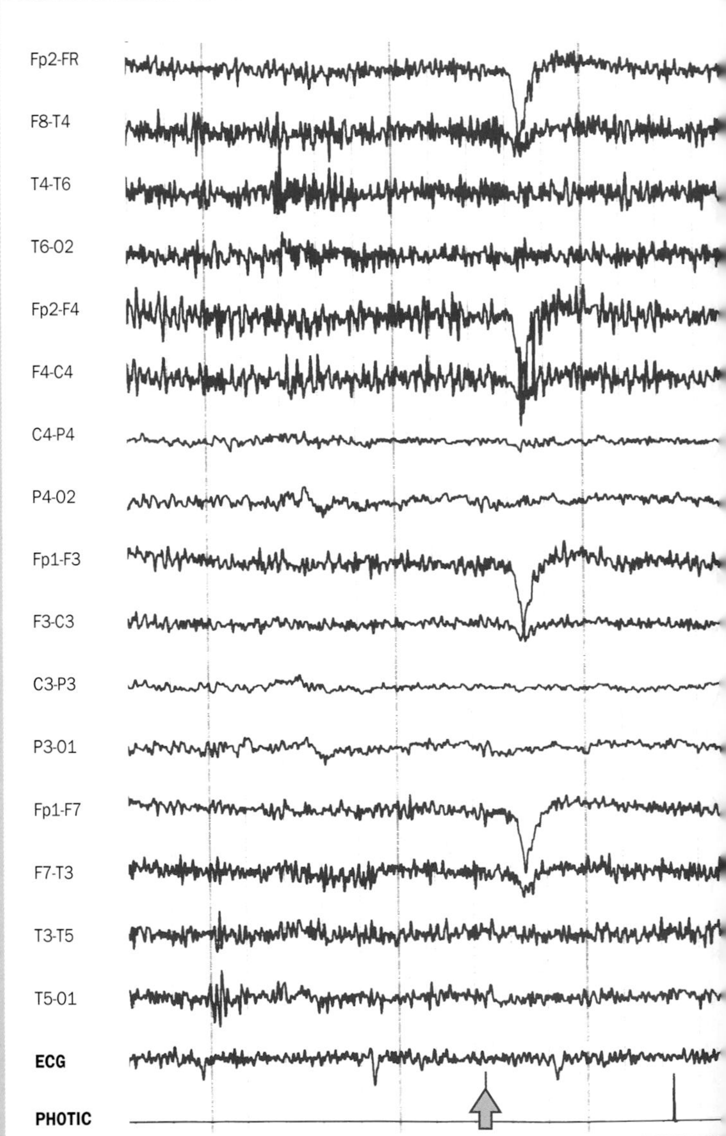

Figure 12b
Pattern sensitivity (pattern reversal): EEG record. The patient, who is also photosensitive, was at a standard distance from a screen which was presenting her with an image of 4mm vertical black and white stripes which reversed colour every second. The onset is marked on the record with an arrow and the pattern reversal marked by the vertical marks at the bottom of the record. After 3 seconds, a brief burst of generalized activity occurred on the record. The patient was markedly pattern sensitive to both static and reversing images and required advice about using computers.

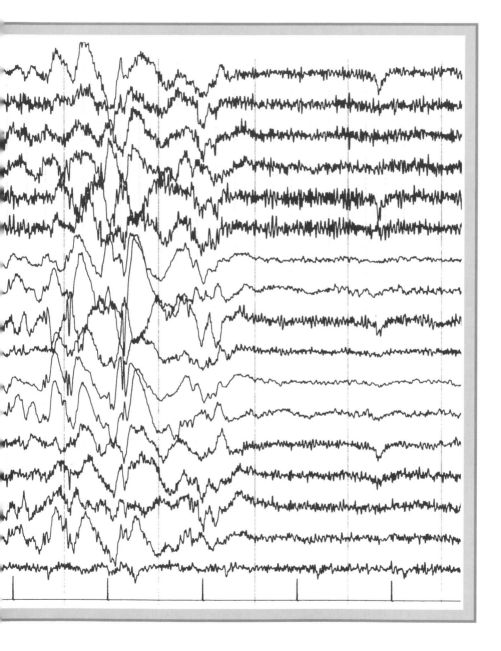

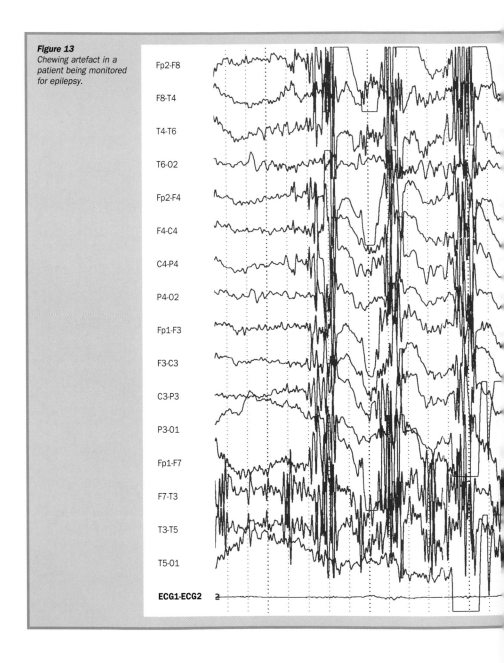

Figure 13
Chewing artefact in a patient being monitored for epilepsy.

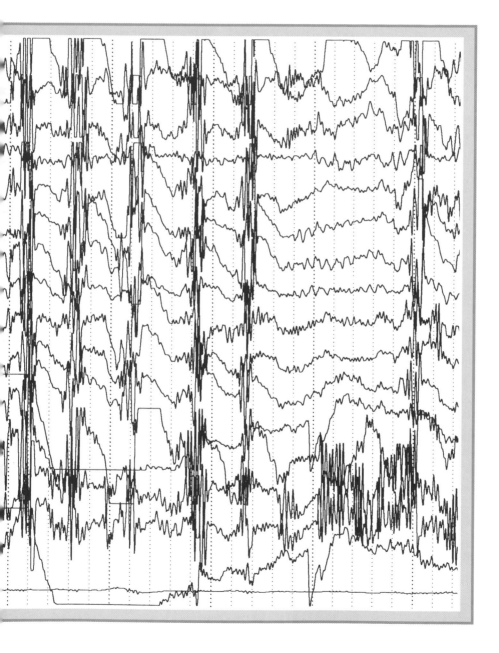

can be used; a time locked EEG signal with video is possible. However, often when a patient is admitted to hospital seizures stop altogether (whether they are epileptic or not). The system is very expensive; muscle and electrode artefact during a seizure somewhat limits the usefulness of this technique although it has the advantage that safe seizure provocation is possible (by drug withdrawal, sleep deprivation or by psychological means — although it is important under such circumstances to be certain that the induced seizures are the same as the patient's usual ones).

Invasive electrode techniques

When it is essential for surgical purposes to localize the source of epileptic discharge accurately and scalp EEG recording does not give a satisfactory result then invasive electrode techniques are used. Electrodes are introduced either through the *foramen ovale* to lie in contact with the base of the temporal lobes or are introduced through the skull to lie in the subdural space on the surface of the brain (*subdural recording*). Occasionally electrodes are inserted into the cortical substance itself. These techniques are not without risk and have a morbidity rate (largely from infection); rarely deaths have occurred, particularly from foramen ovale recording; the help of a neurosurgeon is needed. Invasive tech-

niques should only be used when a positive localization would lead to surgery and only very rarely to identify the provenance of a seizure (although Wyler et al[25] have shown they positively identify epilepsy in patients who, on scalp EEG recording alone, would otherwise have been given a confident diagnosis of non-epileptic seizures).

Magnetoencephalography (MEG)

Chemical events in the brain give off electrical signals; they also give off magnetic signals which can be elaborately converted into digital signals which present samples of magnetic field values produced by neuronal intracellar currents related to transmembrane ion shifts. MEG is probably more accurate than EEG and potentially is an advance in studying the generation and spread of epileptic activity, but its use is limited at the moment by the need to record in a magnetic field free environment and the need to use super conductors (SQUIDS) kept extremely cold at nearly absolute zero.

Imaging

Patients with clinical evidence of partial onset seizures, focal neurological symptoms or signs, or whose epilepsy, although apparently primary generalized, does not come under control swiftly should have cranial MRI imaging (preferably by a high power machine) read by a competent neuroradiologist.

X-ray CT

This has only limited usefulness in epilepsy. Many significant lesions in the aetiology or genesis of epilepsy like neuronal migration defects, some vascular abnormalities and some indolent tumours are unlikely to be visualized on CT and special positions are needed to delineate the temporal lobes. Volumetric analysis of the cranial contents is also impossible. The only advantage of CT over MRI scanning of the brain is that it is easier to see calcification on CT. (A patient suspected of having tuberous sclerosis should certainly have a cranial CT, but even then will also need MRI scanning to determine if any of the tubers are becoming malignant.) CT may be more appropriate in the infant (until myelination has developed). The main disadvantage of CT is that a normal CT scan in a patient who has developed epilepsy, or whose epilepsy has not come under control, is *not* reassuring.

MRI scanning

MRI is the imaging investigation of choice in epilepsy (**Table 11**). It distinguishes between grey and white matter better. Lesions important in epilepsy are revealed on MRI scanning but may not appear on CT scanning (see the section on Neuronal migration defect). Volumetric analysis of the hippocampi is possible (increasingly important in determining the feasibility of temporal lobe surgery). With the right software 'three dimensional' images can be obtained (extremely helpful in determining the extent of cortical lesions). It is possible to undertake *magnetic resonance angiography* without having to inject contrast medium into the carotid arteries — useful in detecting and delineating vascular lesions responsible for epilepsy (**see Figure 14**).[26] A normal, high power, expertly read MRI scan *is* reassuring in new onset epilepsy or in epilepsy which has not come under control. Development of MRI scanning includes functional MRI scanning (using the ability of the MRI to recognize oxyhaemaglobin to measure functional changes in blood flow) and echo planar MRI (which ensures rapid image acquisition) which will be important for epilepsy imaging in the disturbed or uncooperative.[27]

Functional imaging

The place of structural imaging in epilepsy is firmly established. It is also possible nowadays by using radio isotope labelled chemicals to investigate the function of particular parts

Table 11
How to get the best out of an MRI investigation.

1. When requesting an MRI give the radiographer/radiologist as much information as possible (e.g. clinical/EEG localization, significant birth history, history of head injury). If the patient has been imaged before try to provide the previous images for comparison.

2. Indicate what the clinical question is (e.g. is there evidence of unilateral hippocampal sclerosis?). In temporal lobe epilepsy request the cuts that can eventually be used to compare hippocampal volumes on both sides.

3. If clinical history or physical examination suggests the possible presence of a vascular lesion (e.g. migraine and epilepsy together, recurrent transient IIIrd cranial nerve signs) then request magnetic resonance angiography as well — but this is not a routine investigation and leads to longer time in the machine.

4. Prepare the patient for the experience: being placed in the scanner is claustrophobic and it is extremely noisy. The apprehensive may need sedation (10 mg of oral diazepam 2 hours before) and will therefore need an escort. The learning disabled may need I/V sedation or even light anaesthesia; plan the investigation with the radiologist and be able to justify the need for the information the scan will give. A negative scan can have important management implications.

5. Ensure that the experience does not pose undue risk to the patient e.g. early pregnancy, presence of a magnetisable metal in the cranium, orbit or rest of the body (e.g. cardiac pacemakers, sternal wires or artificial hips). Discuss with the radiographer.

6. Remember that an MRI does not measure intelligence, personality or mental state! (Although it may give an explanation for changes in them.)

of the brain (e.g. glucose utilization, binding to receptor sites). This is done either by single photon emission tomography (SPECT) or positron emission tomography (PET) and by the developing technique of MR spectroscopy. Although still deemed experimental, these and similar techniques are likely to become more important in the investigation of epilepsy in the future and already have some part to play in the investigations of patients for possible epilepsy surgery. They may, in years to come, be an essential tool for the investigation of psychiatric disorder in epilepsy and in future drug research.

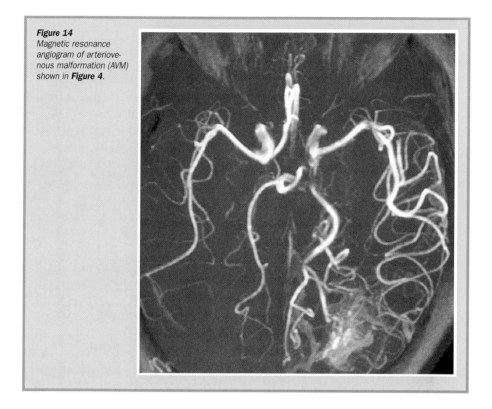

Figure 14
Magnetic resonance angiogram of arteriovenous malformation (AVM) shown in **Figure 4**.

Investigation of the patient with learning disability

Severe intractable epilepsy is much commoner in people with learning disability than in people who are of normal intelligence and who have epilepsy; this disparity is likely to increase so that the difficult to manage epilepsies will largely be found in the learning disabled. The rational management of epilepsy in people with learning difficulty implies good investigation; the need for investigation in people with learning disability with epilepsy is as great, if not greater, than in the non learning disabled. However, people with learning disability and epilepsy are often not fully investigated and are often treated blindly because of perceived difficulty in obtaining such investigation.

There are several reasons for this. Service provision is often directed towards those of normal intelligence and the learning disabled are isolated from such services. There is a perception that people with learning disability do not need good investigation (particularly held by providers of such investigatory services) and there is the problem that the learning disabled, because of difficulties in communication and because of behavioural problems, are sometimes less cooperative and more difficult to keep still. There is an element of truth in the latter but difficulties in communication and behavioural problems should be a challenge to the ingenuity of those who provide investigatory services for people with learning difficulty and not an excuse for inaction or rejection.

EEG investigation is certainly possible in people with learning difficulty but has to be done in an EEG facility which is used to people with learning disability and which has technicians who are prepared to demonstrate the required degrees of patience and tolerance. (It may take patients several visits to the EEG facility to get used to the environment before they will tolerate electrode placement

— modern methods of electrode placement which are neither threatening nor painful are helpful as can be the use of electrode caps, particularly if the wearing of a cap can be presented as some kind of game.) Ambulatory EEG monitoring is possible under close supervision, but, since tolerance of the apparatus may be short in patients with learning disability, investigation should be planned to coincide with the likelihood of maximum seizure activity.

Although some people with learning disability tolerate MRI scanning well it is an unpleasant procedure and many will need sedation or even, occasionally, light anaesthesia in an MRI scanner where continued observation of the patient is possible. It is worthwhile making a decision as to whether or not to sedate or anaesthetize with the radiologist *before* the patient arrives for his scanning appointment. The development of echo planar MRI (with a very rapid acquisition of the signal) will revolutionize the use of MRI scanning in the learning disabled and in psychogeriatrics.

The use of cheap portable video cameras with which carers can videotape apparent seizure activity for later analysis is an extremely important development in learning disability epilepsy. What is now needed is the development of a system of analysis of paroxysmal behaviours in the learning disabled plus a great deal of carer education about the need for proper observation of seizures.

It is also important that the learning disabled have access to facilities for good metabolic and genetic studies. Genetic knowledge is advancing so rapidly that one cannot expect physicians working with the learning disabled to keep up; they must be able to have ready access to colleagues working in genetics.

Further reading

Fish D (1995) The role of electroencephalography. In: *Epilepsy* (eds A Hopkins, S Shorvon and G Cascino). London: Chapman & Hall Medical.

Henry T (1996) Functional neuroimaging with positron emission tomography. *Epilepsia* **37**: 1141–54.

Matthews P, Andermann F and Arnold D (1990) A proton magnetic resonance spectroscopy study of focal epilepsy in humans. *Neurology* **40**: 985–89.

Stefan H, Schneider S, Abraham-Fuchs K et al (1990) Magnetic source localisation in focal epilepsy. *Brain* **113**: 1347–59.

Weiser H (1994) PET and SPECT in epilepsy. *Eur Neurol* **34** (Suppl 1): 58–62.

Treatment

At the end of the investigatory process the diagnosis will
have been confirmed, the seizure type of the patient determined and, sometimes, the cause of the epilepsy recognized.
The physician will have decided if an epilepsy syndrome is
present and can make decisions about treatment.

The aim of treatment is complete control of seizures with
few or no side effects: any side effects must be acceptable to
the patient (rather than to the doctor). There is evidence that
prognosis is better both for seizures and for associated disability if control of seizures can be achieved within 2 years of
seizure onset. Controlling seizures leads to improvement in
quality of life scores,[28] although it is possible, unless the
social and psychological handicaps of epilepsy are managed
pari passu with the seizures, that control over seizures on its
own may have very little effect on the patient's life and
morale. Any treatment programme must be directed as much
at the social and psychological handicaps of epilepsy as at the
seizures themselves.

Full seizure control, however, may not be possible (particularly in the learning disabled) and a policy of damage limitation may be needed, e.g. the elimination of drop attacks rather than other seizures. Control may be obtained at too high a price, so crippling the patient with drug related side effects as to make life intolerable. Some patients, too, may not wish for treatment either because their seizures are so minimal or so infrequent that they feel treatment is not justified or for other personal reasons (often related to fear of side effects or fear of being labelled — adolescents, in particular, are often initially reluctant to take medication).

It is the patient's choice whether to have treatment or not, but since epilepsy is a condition with a definite morbidity (which, if it continues, also carries severe social and psychological handicap) and also has a definite mortality rate,[20] then the decision not to try treatment may have unfortunate consequences. I believe it is a physician's duty to inform a person with newly acquired seizures about the possibility of accidental death in a seizure and the risk of sudden death in epilepsy (perhaps 1/200 per calender year), although this is not a view shared by all clinicians.

Drug treatment (Table 12)

At the moment the basis of the treatment of epilepsy is medical — drug treatment is not curative, although if control is maintained for long enough it is often possible to withdraw the medication slowly without the seizures returning (see later). Drugs need to be taken continually, even though seizures are occasional, (it is *sometimes* possible to treat clusters of seizures or predictable seizures intermittently). The aim is to maintain a steady state blood level of the drug without causing toxic symptoms. This requires good compliance with the medication on the part of the patient — since patchy compliance may actually be more dangerous than not taking medication at all.

Good compliance can only be achieved by cooperation between doctor and patient (the physician explaining why compliance is necessary and setting a simple drug regime which it is possible for the patient to follow; no anticonvulsant drug should be given, except in very unusual circumstances, more than twice a day). In drugs with short half lives (like carbamazepine) sustained release preparations should be used. Careful monitoring of side effects is also necessary; doses

Table 12
Anticonvulsant drugs.

Drug	Year introduced
Phenobarbitone	1912
Phenytoin	1938
Primidone	1952
Ethosuximide	1960
Carbamazepine	1963
Clonazepam	1974
Sodium valproate	1974
Clobazam	1982
Vigabatrin	1989
Lamotrigine	1991
Gabapentin	1993
Topiramate	1995
Tiagabine	1997 ?

should be adjusted to achieve the maximum of seizure control with the minimum of side effects. Most troublesome side effects with anticonvulsant drugs are neurotoxic (headache, nausea, vomiting, sedation, cognitive impairment, ataxia and double vision). They may be a price that the patient is not willing to pay for seizure control, particularly if alternative treatments are available.

Blood level monitoring

It has become the fashion to measure blood levels of anticonvulsant drugs where possible in order to determine the effective dose. Apart from phenytoin (where blood level monitoring is mandatory) blood level monitoring is usually not necessary and may lead to unnecessary increases in dosage of a drug when the patient has already achieved seizure control or to unneeded reduction in a dose which has achieved seizure control when side effects were not occurring, so that seizures return (this is particularly likely to occur with carbamazepine, sodium valproate and lamotrigine).

Serum level monitoring may occasionally be used to detect or confirm poor compliance with medication or rarely to confirm possible drug toxicity; occasionally in patients undergoing reappraisal of treatment who are taking several drugs blood levels of the anticonvulsants are helpful in determining which drug to withdraw first. Rarely serum concentrations of lamotrigine are a useful guide when withdrawing patients from concomitant valproate. It should be remembered that:

1. Routine clinical methods of drug estimation do not determine free as opposed to bound levels of the drug in the bloodstream (a potential problem when measuring serum levels of phenytoin in patients also taking sodium valproate when the blood level of phenytoin may be erroneously reassuring — valproate increases the unbound fraction of phenytoin).

2. Levels of the metabolite of a drug, which are not routinely measured, may be more important (such as carbamazepine epoxide). It is possible to have a patient with 'normal' carbamazepine levels who is yet intoxicated by the metabolite, levels of which have not been measured.

3. There may be an argument in old people for measuring serum levels since they often achieve higher serum concentrations with lower doses of antiepileptic drugs.

4. People with severe learning difficulty who lack verbal skills and who cannot report their side effects may need drug level monitoring to avoid inadvertent intoxication (some laboratories have facilities for measuring saliva concentrations of drugs, thus avoiding frequent blood sampling). However, the observations of skilled carers are equally important in determining whether intoxication is present.

Initial therapy (Table 13)

Having decided (after consultation) to treat with medication (because the patient's seizures are severe enough, and are potentially life threatening and are clearly going to continue without treatment) the physician should introduce one of the first line drugs. The initial dose should be small, the dose regimen should be no more than twice a day, increase in dosage should be gradual and should stop when it is clear that the seizures have come under control. In this way side effects are often avoided (particularly neurotoxic side effects and rash). Too rapid an escalation often leads to the patient taking far more of the drug than he or she actually needs and with unnecessary over sedation. There is controversy (which ought to be resolved) as to whether or not anticonvulsant drugs have a **therapeutic window** and that higher than necessary doses of anticonvulsants can actually create the very condition they are meant to control, but clinical experience suggests that this may be so particularly in patients with learning difficulty; unfortunately dropping the dose back to the level at which seizures had originally been controlled

may not restore control. Dose increases should be driven by lack of seizure control, but neither by blood levels (except with phenytoin) nor belief in the usual dose of a drug.

The choice of the first line drug may depend on the type of epilepsy that the patient has. For most adolescent and adult patients evidence based medicine suggests that lamotrigine (despite its potentially increased cost) may be the first line drug of choice in patients with partial onset epilepsy.[29] It is certainly as effective as carbamazepine with a significantly lower side effect profile. This is also true for gabapentin where recent monotherapy trials have shown equal efficacy to carbamazepine with a lower side effect

Table 13
First line drugs.

A. Lamotrigine

B. Carbamazepine[*,†,§,¶]

C. Sodium valproate[†,‡,¶]

D. Gabapentin[*]

* Avoid in proven primary generalized epilepsy

† Primary generalized epilepsy (all types) only

‡ Best avoided in women of childbearing potential

§ Prescribe in sustained release form

¶ Avoid generics

profile. Gabapentin's lack of interaction with other medication may be especially valuable.[30] Head to head trials against lamotrigine in first line monotherapy are taking place.

In primary generalized epilepsy sodium valproate is usually regarded as the first line drug (although this is not actually based on clinical trial data). Lamotrigine may be as effective as sodium valproate in the primary generalized epilepsies (although there are no formal clinical trial data to substantiate this). In women in particular because of the known teratogenic side effects of sodium valproate, lamotrigine might be considered to be preferable as a first line drug — this is debateable although it is Birmingham Brainwave's policy to use lamotrigine as its first line drug in all forms of epilepsy. In view of its broad spectrum of activity and, if used with a low slow dose escalation, its better side effect profile, lamotrigine certainly should be considered the first line drug in people with learning disability: in patients with learning difficulty with known partial onset seizures gabapentin is also a first line drug.

Whatever first line drug is used about 70–80% of patients will become controlled; most will remain controlled and can be returned to general practice supervision with an agreed plan for re-referral if necessary. Patients who do not achieve full control are more likely to have concomitant physical problems, brain damage, learning difficulty or personality problems (leading to poor compliance).

Management of the chronic patient

8

If seizures have not come under control with medication within 2 years of onset, there is a diminishing chance that they will and the patient can be considered to have chronic epilepsy. Such patients need regular review so that they can benefit from the rapid advances being made in epilepsy care. In the course of their work psychiatrists may see patients who continue to have seizures despite treatment; the regimen outlined below for managing chronic epilepsy and for initiating drug changes should be known to them. This is certainly true of psychiatrists working in learning disability, but should also be true for general psychiatrists (who occasionally adopt a rather passive helpless attitude when faced by patients with epilepsy). The principles of management are simple and are well within their competence. Patients should not be dumped onto the local neurologist who may have little interest in managing them. There is a general problem (in people with epilepsy themselves, in their general practitioners and, sadly, in some specialists) of a low expectation of control in epilepsy: far too many patients who continue to have seizures are regarded as either being controlled or as beyond further help when, in fact, they are not.[31]

Some patients with chronic epilepsy, if reinvestigated, turn out not to have epilepsy but some kind of non epileptic seizure disorder (see the section on Is it really epilepsy?). No matter who has made the original diagnosis and no matter what authority they have, when reassessing the chronic patient one should always find out how the diagnosis of epilepsy had been made and, if necessary, institute special investigations like video EEG telemetry to establish the diagnosis with certainty **(Table 14)**.

It is often apparent on reviewing a patient's treatment that although appropriate first line

Table 14
Management of the chronic patient — general review points.

1. *Is this really epilepsy?*
2. *If it is, has it been classified correctly?*
3. *Is there an unrecognized epilepsy syndrome?*
4. *Has the appropriate first line therapy been tried to the limits of tolerance?*
5. *Is there a compliance problem?*
6. *Is there evidence of learning difficulty, physical handicap or mental illness?*
7. *Is there a significant psychological problem?*
8. ***Review previous investigations***
9. *Is there previously unsuspected cerebral disease?*
10. *Consider full reinvestigation*
11. *Consider a surgical option*
12. *Develop a management plan with second line and third line drugs*
13. *Consider psychological therapy*
14. *Any special features (e.g. reflex, clusters, premenstrual)?*
15. *If all reasonable drugs tried, is the patient suitable for a drug trial?*
16. *If all therapy has failed and diagnosis of epilepsy still certain consider special treatments like diet, or complementary therapies or consider slowly withdrawing all medication*

therapy has been tried, attempts at treatment were abandoned prematurely, often for illogical or irrational reasons (if they were abandoned because of intolerable side effects that is a good reason). It is important to ensure that patients have tried the full appropriate first line treatment for their particular form of epilepsy **(see Table 13)**. There may be exceptions to this rule with carbamazepine and valproate if the patient is a woman who is intending to become pregnant.

If first line drugs have been tried to the full then second line drugs are appropriate but it would be worthwhile checking first of all that the patient was actually compliant with the first line medication (some patients, particularly adolescents, just do not take their medication properly and this needs to be addressed). Patients with learning disability or with physical handicap are less likely to get full control and the clinician may have to be thinking more in terms of damage limitation (i.e. controlling drop attacks rather than absences). Significant mental illness in the patient may lead to difficulty with compliance.

Psychological problems may be perpetuating the seizures, even though they are genuine epileptic ones, particularly in patients who are very anxious, if there is a family crisis and family anxiety is increasing seizure frequency or, as not uncommonly happens, genuine epileptic seizures are receiving secondary gain and the patient has a need to maintain disability. It would be no use trying to change medication unless these issues had been first addressed.

It is important to review previous investigations which may have been inadequate (e.g. no appropriate EEG investigation, CT scanning rather than MRI, etc) in case the patient has a lesion like a cavernous haemangioma or unilateral hippocampal sclerosis where a surgical option would be more appropriate. It is often necessary to fully reinvestigate the patient at this stage including up-to-date MRI scanning, ictal EEG recording, etc, particularly because in patients with partial onset seizures (who are the bulk of patients with chronic epilepsy) the surgical option should be seriously considered. One of the problems in management is that the results of previous investigations are often impossible to obtain: since very few patients (or their GPs) are ever told what the results of investigations were, costly reinvestigation may have to be done purely because of inadequate records.

If the surgical option is not likely to help (see the section on surgical treatment) then a management plan should be developed with the appropriate second (and if necessary third) line drug **(see Tables 15–18)**. Choices

differ: the reader may consider the plans outlined in **Tables 15–18** a little idiosyncratic
but they are based on two treatment principles which I consider important:

1. **The mode of action of the chosen drug,
   if known**. If the first failed drug, for
   instance, inhibits sodium transport then
   the second drug chosen should, if possible, have a different mode of action (e.g.
   enhancing GABA release); the first drug
   should not usually be replaced with one
   which has a similar mode of action.

2. **In considering a replacement drug
   some consideration should be given to
   its potential side effect profile**. Some
   drugs are more teratogenic than others, a
   consideration in women, some are more
   sedating and likely to cause cognitive
   impairment and some, undoubtedly, are
   more prone to cause depression and psychosis. Such considerations are important
   in all patients but particularly in the learning disabled and those with a history of
   mental illness.

Sometimes there are special features to the
patient's seizures (e.g. they are reflex, see
the section on reflex epilepsies) and they
are therefore amenable to other forms of

treatment or they may reliably cluster so
that short-term therapy with clobazam
can be considered, or they may occur at a
specific time in the menstrual cycle (in
which case, again, short-term therapy with
clobazam may be very helpful), or hor-
monal treatment might be considered (see
the section on women and epilepsy).
Psychological therapy can be effective (see
the section on the psychological treatment
of epilepsy) and should be considered as
part of the treatment plan and not used as
a last resort at the very end after an
exhaustive trawl through all available drug
therapies.

If most therapies which are likely to benefit (and not do harm) have been considered, rejected or tried then the patient
may well be suitable for a drug trial: several interesting compounds are in active
stages of development at the moment. If
all therapy has failed then the use of some
of the alternative or complementary therapies (see the sections on alternative therapy) may be considered. In some resistant
epilepsies of adolescence, particularly the
Lennox–Gastaut syndrome, a ketogenic
diet may be a possibility. Sometimes, if all
else fails, a *slow*, careful withdrawal of
medication may be appropriate. There is

Table 15
Second line drugs primary generalized (depending on which was used first).

A. Lamotrigine *

B. Sodium valproate *,†,‡

* There is an interaction between lamotrigine and valproate: if lamotrigine is being added to valproate use very small doses initially (say 5–10 mg daily) and if valproate is later withdrawn the dose of lamotrigine will need to be increased. When adding valproate to lamotrigine be prepared to drop the dose of lamotrigine if neurotoxic side effects appear

† Consider avoiding this drug in women of childbearing potential

‡ Avoid generics

Table 16
Second line drugs (partial onset) depending on which was used first.

A. Gabapentin *

B. Lamotrigine

C. Carbamezipine *,†,‡,§

D. Tiagabine (when available) *

* Avoid in proven primary generalized epilepsy

† Avoid in women of childbearing potential if possible

‡ Use sustained release formulation

§ Avoid generics

Table 17
Third line drugs (primary generalized).

Drugs to be considered if first and second line have failed
A. Ethosuximide (absences only)
B. Clonazepam
C. Levetiracetam (UCB L059) (when available)
D. Piracetam (myoclonus only)
E. Clobazam (if clusters, situational or menstrually related)
Note: occasionally drugs considered more suitable for partial onset may be tried (especially gabapentin or topiramate) but are unlikely to control absences or myoclonic jerks; carbamazepine and vigabatrin may make myoclonic jerks worse

Table 18
Third line drugs (partial onset).

Drugs to be considered if first and second line have failed
A. Topiramate[†]
B. Clonazepam
C. Clobazam (if clusters, situational or menstrually related)
D. Vigabatrin*
E. Phenytoin[†]
F. Phenobarbitone[†]
* See the section on this drug
† Avoid in women of childbearing potential if possible

no point in taking medication for an epilepsy which is resistant to it: sometimes withdrawal of medication leads to lessening of seizure frequency for reasons which are not understood.

In people with learning difficulty or mental illness, consideration has to be given to any potential interaction between the chosen anticonvulsant and medication that the patient may already be taking (e.g. antidepressants, antipsychotic drugs, drugs to control movement disorder or to control behavioural outbursts). By and large anticonvulsants which are not enzyme inducing, which are not known to be likely to produce or exacerbate mental illness or behavioural changes, are more appropriate for the learning disabled or mentally ill (e.g. lamotrigine, gabapentin, sodium valproate).

Monotherapy versus polytherapy

Most patients with chronic epilepsy end up on two or more anticonvulsants: there has been controversy in the epilepsy world for a long time about whether two anticonvulsants are ever better than one. This remains a disputed area but there are certain important guiding principles.

1. *Most* patients will manage on monotherapy, when adding in a second drug to a failed first drug, when an appropriate dose has been reached (rarely guided by blood level monitoring — this may be important occasionally such as when adding lamotrigine to valproate) then, assuming better seizure control has been reached, the first drug should be *slowly* withdrawn with adjustments of dose of the second drug if necessary (i.e. increasing the lamotrigine dose as one withdraws valproate). Patients who have achieved seizure control for the first time may be reluctant to do this and, if they are not too troubled by side effects, may choose to end up on polytherapy. If one adds in a second drug and it is successful it is important to wait a few months before initiating slow withdrawal of the first **(see Table 19 for withdrawal schedules)**.

2. There is some evidence that two drugs may sometimes work better together than each individually. This is particularly likely to be so in patients who have more than one type of seizure, who may need two drugs with different mode of actions (i.e. it might be logical to combine a sodium transport inhibiting drug with a GABA enhancing drug under certain cir-

cumstances — there might be less point in combining two sodium transport inhibitor drugs or two GABA enhancing drugs).

Although it does happen, there should really be no excuse for using three drugs: if adding in a third to a failed twosome you should always try to withdraw one of them (although you may encounter patient resistance). Blood level monitoring may help to determine which is likely to be the least effective drug.

With each succeeding drug addition the chances of full seizure control lessen. There are exceptions to this rule (for instance, when an epilepsy syndrome has been treated with the wrong medication, e.g. juvenile myoclonic epilepsy treated with carbamazepine or vigabatrin). Some drugs are being developed, or have recently arrived, either with multiple modes of action or with unique modes of action which may improve this rather bleak prognosis.

For practical advice about which drugs to add, in what order, see the accompanying tables **(15–18)** and also the information about individual drugs. It is important to remember that the advice given here is biased towards a learning difficulty population and is based partly on evidence based medicine but also on extensive clinical experience. Different authorities will have different views, but different authorities are working from separate databases of experience.

See specialized texts for practical advice about the management of epilepsy in children (the advice given here would be correct from the age of 12 onwards)[6] and the management of epilepsy in the elderly.[32]

Drug withdrawal

In the majority of patients who have been seizure free for 5 years drug withdrawal can be attempted providing it is done slowly **(see Table 19 on drug withdrawal)**. If the patient is comfortable with the drug, has no important side effects and seizure return would be devastating (e.g. loss of driving licence) then withdrawal need not be forced on the patient. Relapse of controlled epilepsy even when the patient is on anticonvulsants is quite common (10–20%). After 5 years in most patients relapse becomes independent of whether or not the patient is taking medication. Factors influencing relapse are shown in **Table 20.[33] Prognosis for withdrawal may be better in children but there is not complete agreement on this. If seizures**

Table 19
Birmingham Brainwave: suggested withdrawal regimens for anticonvulsants (outpatient schedule). These regimens assume that the patient is taking another effective anticonvulsant. If monotherapy withdrawal is being practised then double the withdrawal time (e.g. monthly becomes every two months, fortnightly becomes monthly).

Primidone	125 mg monthly
Phenobarbitone	15 mg monthly
Phenytoin	25 mg fortnightly
Ethosuximide	125 mg monthly
Carbamazepine	100 mg fortnightly
Sodium valproate *	200/300 mg monthly
Clobazam[†]	10 mg monthly: take last dose on alternate days for 2 weeks
Clonazepam[†]	0.25 mg fortnightly
Lamotrigine	$\frac{1}{4}$ of dose fortnightly
Gabapentin	$\frac{1}{4}$ of dose fortnightly
Vigabatrin	500 mg monthly
Topiramate	$\frac{1}{4}$ of dose fortnightly

* *There is empirical evidence that primary generalized seizures may return many months after monotherapy withdrawal of this drug: it may be advisable to check an EEG at 6 months and 12 months post withdrawal (including photosensitivity)*

† *Withdrawal may lead to rebound anxiety symptoms and may need to be covered by diminishing doses of diazepam (as with lorazepam). 10 mg tablets are now available of clobazam, which can be broken in half so that 5 mg dose reductions are possible*

return there is no guarantee that re-starting treatment will lead to control again.

The decision to withdraw from medication should be thoroughly discussed with the patient. In patients with learning difficulty it is important not to continue potentially intoxicating drugs unnecessarily and it is particularly important to avoid polypharmacy. It is likely (although not proven) that with-

Table 20
(a) Factors associated with good prognosis on anticonvulsant withdrawal.[33]

1. Long duration of remission
2. Brief epileptic history
3. Rapid remission with treatment

(b) Factors associated with poor prognosis on anticonvulsant withdrawal

1. Age 16 or older
2. Taking more than one anti-epileptic drug
3. Seizures after the start of anti-epileptic drug treatment
4. History of primary or secondary generalized tonic-clonic seizures
5. History of myoclonic seizures
6. Abnormal EEG in past year

drawal of all medication in patients with severe brain lesions or with metabolic causes for their epilepsy is more likely to lead to a return of seizures and full withdrawal (as opposed to rationalizing to monotherapy) should be done very cautiously. Some anti-convulsant medications (e.g. carbamazepine, possibly lamotrigine and certainly benzodiazepines) have psychotropic effects: withdrawal of these drugs may lead to return of anxiety, a mood disorder or behavioural disturbance.

Anti-epileptic drugs

When prescribing an unfamiliar anti-epileptic drug, it is important that the British National Formulary or data sheet is read. However, clinical practice and experience may lead to eventual deviations from data sheet recommendations. The patient should also be encouraged to read the information leaflet provided in the drug pack.

Acetazolamide	
Trade name:	*Diamox*
Mode(s) of action:	*weak diuretic, carbonic anhydrase inhibitor*
Indications:	*add on, particularly for menstrually related seizures (partial onset), anecdotally effective against absences and myoclonic jerks*
Dose:	*250–1000 mg daily in divided doses*
'Therapeutic range':	*Not measured*
Side effects, dose related:	*Fatigue, headache, tinnitus, parathesiae, metabolic acidosis*
Hypersensitivity:	*Leucopenia, thombocytopenia, aplastic anaemia, rash including Stevens–Johnson syndrome*
Chronic toxicity:	*Hypokalaemia, acidosis, may worsen closed angle glaucoma*
Teratogenic:	*Yes (animal data)*
Advantages:	*Useful for predictable clusters, menstrually related seizures*
Disadvantages:	*Effect wears off; unpleasant side effects*

Carbamazepine

Trade name:	Tegretol, Tegretol Retard (sustained release form), several generics
Mode(s) of action:	Limits repetitive firing of Na^+ dependent action potentials
Indications:	First line partial, partial with secondary generalization, primary generalized tonic clonic
Contraindications:	Primary generalized absences, myoclonic jerks
Dose:	Initial dose 100 mg nocte 2/52 then increment of 100 mg 2/52 until seizures stop or 400 mg b.d. is reached. Dose can go higher but likely to cause unacceptable side effects. **Avoid generics**
'Therapeutic range':	4–12 µg/ml (but some patients have neurotoxic side effects well below the upper range and some can, without side effects, greatly exceed it)
Side-effects, dose related:	Dizziness, diplopia, ataxia, nausea, vomiting, headache and some cognitive impairment
Hypersensitivity:	Rash (avoid with low slow dose escalation), including Stevens–Johnson, leucopaenia (which can cause alarm): possible multi-organ failure
Chronic toxicity:	Low serum sodium, sometimes symptomatic, affects thyroid function tests
Teratogenic:	Yes (animal and human data) women of childbearing potential should take folic acid (5 mg daily) while taking carbamazepine
Advantages:	Mood stabilizer
Disadvantages:	Enzyme induction (large number of drug interactions including contraceptive pill). Subtle but definite cognitive side effects

Note: Dosage recommendation is not that of data sheet but is based on clinical experience (particularly of learning disability population). The data sheet also recommends weekly then monthly blood counts, but few doctors do this

Clobazam

Trade name:	Frisium (S3B)
Mode(s) of action:	GABA mediated inhibition via benzodiazepine receptor (often short lived)
Indications:	Short-term breaking up of seizure clusters or for premenstrual exacerbations
Contraindications:	Previous benzodiazepine dependence
Dose:	10–60 mg a day, once or twice daily; start with 10 mg daily and titrate dose against effect; do not use for more than 10–14 days at a time. (Capsules are being replaced with tablets which are scored to allow 5 mg doses to be used; useful in withdrawal of drug)
'Therapeutic range':	Not measured
Side effects dose related:	Drowsiness, sedation, rarely disinhibition
Hypersensitivity:	Rare rash
Chronic toxicity:	Unknown, but dependence possible; loss of effect with chronic dosage usual (but rarely chronic use leads to permanent control of seizures)
Teratogenic:	Probably not
Advantages:	Useful as a 'rescue' remedy
Disadvantages:	Those of all benzodiazepines: loss of effect; on NHS 'blacklist'. Can be prescribed for epilepsy under 'Schedule 3B' — so put 'S3B' after prescription

Clonazepam

Trade name:	Rivitrol
Mode(s) of action:	GABA mediated inhibition via benzodiazepine receptor
Indications:	Resistant primary generalized seizures, particularly absences; myoclonic: sometimes partial onset, third-line therapy. **Very useful in status epilepticus i/v**
Contraindications:	Previous benzodiazepine dependence; use cautiously in patients with learning disability

Cont'd.

Dose:	0.5–8 mg total daily dose; start with 0.5 mg at night and titrate dose against side effects and control of seizures
'Therapeutic range':	Not measured
Side effects, dose related:	Sedation, drowsiness, drooling, irritability, disinhibition
Hypersensitivity:	Rare rash
Chronic toxicity:	Dependence
Teratogenic:	Possibly, uncertain
Advantages:	Useful in resistant primary general epilepsy and in status
Disadvantages:	Dependence, sedation, loss of effect (?less than with clobazam). Toxic dose (sedation) very close to effective dose, making titration difficult

Note: Read instructions carefully when using i/v

Diazepam	
Trade name:	Valium (Diazemuls (i.v.), stesolid (rectal))
Mode(s) of action	GABA mediated inhibition via benzodiazepine receptor (short lived)
Indications:	Status epilepticus (i.v., rectal). Orally, limited use as one-off rescue remedy (as clobazam)
Contraindications:	(For status) use cautiously in patients with known respiratory difficulty or aggressive outbursts
Dose:	(i.v.) use diazemuls if possible: slow (5 mg/min) injection of 10–20 mg (adults); may be repeated (but be wary of accumulation with respiratory depression). (Rectal) 10–30 mg (adults), may be repeated (but be wary of accumulation with respiratory depression)
'Therapeutic range':	Not measured
Side effects dose related:	Sedation, accumulation on repeated dose, respiratory depression, hypotension
Hypersensitivity:	Rare rash

Chronic toxicity:	Dependence
Teratogenic:	Possibly
Advantages:	(i.v.: rectal), safest treatment for status epilepticus which usually works
Disadvantage:	Sedation, respiratory depression, accumulation, possible dependence; rectal route raises ethical issues; intravenous route risks extravasation with skin necrosis

Note: All patients in status epilepticus should be admitted to hospital for observation even if apparently controlled by i/v diazepam in the community. If status epilepticus does not stop the patient must be admitted to an ITU

Ethosuximide	
Trade name:	Zarontin
Mode(s) of action:	Uncertain; reduces Ca^{++} flux
Indications:	Primary general absences only
Dose:	Up to 2 g total daily dose
'Therapeutic range':	40–100 µg/ml
Side effects, dose related:	Nausea, sedation, headache, psychosis, may induce tonic clonic seizures
Hypersensitivity:	Rash, leucopenia
Chronic toxicity:	None known
Teratogenic:	Yes (human data). Women of child bearing potential should take 5 mg folic acid daily (but this may not be protective)
Advantages:	Specific for absences
Disadvantages:	Limited use; has a reputation for inducing tonic clonic seizures in patients with absences (?undeserved)

Felbamate

Trade name:	Not currently licensed in UK, but can be used on named patient basis if clinician accepts responsibility
Mode(s) of action:	Unknown
Indications:	Severe drug resistant partial epilepsies; Lennox–Gastaut syndrome
Dose:	1200–3600 mg total daily dose
'Therapeutic range':	Not measured
Side effects, dose related:	Sedation, insomnia, weight loss, nausea
Hypersensitivity:	Aplastic anaemia; liver failure
Chronic toxicity:	Unknown
Teratogenic:	Unknown
Advantages:	Sometimes works when nothing else does
Disadvantages:	Potentially fatal liver and marrow toxicity. Causes **increase** in phenytoin/valproate levels; **fall** in carbamazepine level (but **increase** in carbamazepine epoxide levels), risk of acute intoxication, large number of irritating side effects

Gabapentin

Trade name:	Neurontin
Mode(s) of action:	Unknown; effects on amino acid transport or on second messenger mechanisms, or indirect effect on GABA or glutamate receptors have all been postulated
Indications:	Partial onset seizures, with or without secondary generalization; evidence is accumulating that it is likely to be an appropriate first line drug for this indication. Its place in primary generalized epilepsy is uncertain; the only controlled trial probably used too low a dose and there have been anecdotal reports of success

Dose:	Fast escalation is possible (see data sheet) but usually start with 400 mg at night: increase the dose by fortnightly increments of 400 mg (using a twice daily regimen) until seizures controlled or dose of 2400 reached: if appreciable but not complete effect consider further increase to 3600–4800 mg total daily dose. Early studies with this drug pitched the suggested dose too low. Twice daily doseage (despite data sheet) seems effective and is much more convenient but use thrice daily dose at high dose levels if necessary to avoid dose dependent side effects
'Therapeutic range':	Not tested
Side effects, dose related:	Sedation, dizziness, nausea, ataxia, possible worsening of seizures (unproven)
Hypersensitivity:	None described
Chronic toxicity:	None reported
Teratogenic:	Probably not ('clean' animal data)
Advantages:	Low side effect profile; more effective than originally reported (with the right dose); no interactions. Rapid escalation is possible (but not routinely recommended)
Disadvantages:	Possible need for thrice daily dosage: effective dose higher than originally expected

Note: Dosage recommendations are not those of the data sheet, but are based on audited experience

Lamotrigine	
Trade name:	Lamictal
Mode(s) of action:	Inhibits pathological release of glutamate by acting on fast sodium channels
Indications:	First line monotherapy for partial seizures with or without secondary generalization. Clinical experience strongly suggests efficacy in primary generalized epilepsy and therefore, like valproate, a broad spectrum anticonvulsant. Licensed for the Lennox–Gastaut syndrome and particularly effective in atypical absences

Cont'd.

Dose:	*Depends on concomitant medication: in initial monotherapy or when added to valproate in monotherapy or to a non enzyme inducer in monotherapy need only be taken once a day. Start with 10 mg daily for 2 weeks then 25 mg daily for a month; thereafter monthly increments of 25 mg to 100 mg daily. If added to valproate in monotherapy ceiling dose is probably 200 mg daily, otherwise maximum dose is 600–800 mg daily. If added to an enzyme inducing drug start with 25 mg daily then 25 mg increments (using twice daily regimens) fortnightly (depends on effect) until 400–600 mg total daily dose is reached if seizures continue. If added to carbamazepine reduction in dose of carbamazepine will be needed if neurotoxic side effects appear*
'Therapeutic range':	*There is no relationship between serum level and side effects or therapeutic efficacy; the quoted range of 1–4 µg/ml was plucked out of the air and is far too low. Serum level estimation is useful whilst withdrawing valproate*
Side effects, dose related:	*Rash — potentially serious, almost always avoided by low slow dose introduction and increments. More likely to happen if valproate being used without an enzyme inducing drug and possibly more likely in children under 12. Neurotoxic side effects (ataxia, diplopia, headache, vomiting) are dose dependent (there is a pharmacodynamic interaction between lamotrigine and carbamazepine so if these side effects appear reduce concomitant carbamazepine rather than lamotrigine)*
Hypersensitivity:	*Rash (dose dependent — see above), possible acute hepatic dysfunction or multi-organ failure (not proven), probably seizure related*
Chronic toxicity:	*None described*
Teratogenic:	*Unlikely ('clean' animal data)*
Advantages:	*Low (or avoidable) side effect profile: enhances mood and feelings of well being, does not impair cognitive function, an ideal monotherapy drug*
Disadvantages:	*Dose cannot be escalated quickly because of hypersensitivity rash, interactions with other AEDs (particularly valproate which inhibits its metabolism) makes adding on lamotrigine slightly tricky*

Levetiracetam

Trade name:	Not yet on market: code name is UCB L059
Mode(s) of action:	Unknown, s-enantioner of piracetam, effective in resistant cortical myoclonus
Indications:	Add on for resistant partial seizures with or without secondary generalization, anecdotally effective in resistant primary generalization
Dose:	Probably between 1 g and 4 g daily
'Therapeutic range':	Undecided
Side effects, dose related:	Sedation, insomnia, possible rash
Hypersensitivity:	None reported
Chronic toxicity:	None reported
Teratogenic:	Unknown (possibly not)
Advantages:	Trials so far suggest effective drug with acceptable side effects profile, may be particularly helpful with resistant primary generalized epilepsy including myoclonic jerks
Disadvantages:	As yet not known.This drug is not yet on the market

Phenobarbitone

Trade names:	Gardenal, Luminal, Prominal
Mode(s) of action:	Enhancement of GABA mediated inhibition
Indications:	(Rarely) partial seizures, with or without secondary generalization, occasional parental use in status epilepticus
Dose:	30–200 mg total daily dose (once daily sufficient unless taking concomitant enzyme inducing drug)
'Therapeutic range':	15–40 µg/ml, probably of little significance, as tolerance occurs
Side effects, dose related:	Sedation, ataxia, cognitive impairment
Hypersensitivity:	Rash
Chronic toxicity:	Megaloblastic anaemia (folate deficiency), osteoporosis (inhibits vitamin D absorption)

Cont'd.

Teratogenic:	Yes. Women of childbearing potential should take folic acid (5 mg daily) while taking this drug
Advantages:	None: a last resort drug
Disadvantages:	Enzyme induction with consequent interactions, side effects

Phenytoin

Trade name:	Epanutin (several generics)
Mode(s) of action:	Limits repetitive firing of Na^+ dependent action potentials
Indications:	Partial onset with or without secondary generalization, possible role in resistant primary generalized, no longer first line, i/v use in status epilepticus
Dose:	200–600 mg daily, once daily dosage acceptable in monotherapy or in absence of other enzyme inducing drugs. **Avoid generics**
'Therapeutic range':	The only drug where serum level monitoring is essential after each dose change as (a) there is a non-linear relationship between dose and serum concentration, and (b) chronic intoxication can be clinically silent until lasting damage has been done to the cerebellum. 10–20 µg/ml: note when 'in' range dose increments should be no more than 25 mg, when 'over' range dose decrements should be no more than 25–50 mg. Serum levels may be 'in range' and yet be toxic if valproate is a concomitant due to decreased protein binding
Side effects, dose related:	Sedation, ataxia, dysarthria, nausea, vomiting
Hypersensitivity:	Rash, pseudo lymphoma, hepatitis
Chronic toxicity	Cerebellar atrophy, osteomalacia, megaloblastic (folate deficient) anaemia, gingival hypertrophy, hirsutism, probable coarsening of facial features if dose over range
Teratogenic:	Yes. Women of childbearing potential should take folic acid (5 mg daily) while taking this drug
Advantages:	Still occasionally useful as it is an effective drug but needs care with dosage
Disadvantages:	Enzyme inducing with numerous drug interactions, long term side effects, non-linear kinetics. Use can only be rarely justified in potentially fertile women

Sodium valproate

Trade name:
use has

Epilim: Epilim Chrono is a 'long acting' variant, but its yet to be justified, several generics

Mode of action:

Uncertain — possibly by acting on GABA ergic neurons

Indications:

First line primary generalized epilepsy, also partial with secondary generalized, specific for photosensitivity

Dose:

400 mg – 3 g total daily dose (once daily in monotherapy or in absence of enzyme inducing drugs). **Avoid generics**

'Therapeutic range':

50–100 mg/ml quoted but fairly meaningless, blood levels over 100 mg/ml are more likely to be associated with toxicity

Side effects, dose related:

Hand tremor, weight gain, irritability, confusion, gastric intolerance

Hypersensitivity:

Hepatotoxicity (mainly young children)

Chronic toxicity:

Hair loss (rarely total), amenorrhoea, polycystic ovary syndrome

Teratogenic:

Yes. If it has to be used in women of childbearing potential, divide daily dose in three and take folic acid (5 mg daily).

Advantages:

Effective, often little effect (in reasonable doses) on cognitive function, specific for photosensitivity, no interactions (except with lamotrigine). If added to lamotrigine neurotoxic side effects may occur and the dose of lamotrigine will need to be reduced

Disadvantages:

Weight gain, teratogenicity and effect on sex hormones

Tiagabine

Trade name:

Gabatril (expected on UK market in 1998)

Mode(s) of action:

Inhibits GABA re-uptake

Indications:

Add-on for partial onset seizures with or without secondary generalization, trials underway both in primary generalized epilepsy and as a first line monotherapy choice

Dose:

See manufacturer's data sheet when drug available, short half life of this drug means thrice daily dosage to avoid side effects

Cont'd.

'Therapeutic range':	Not tested
Side-effects, dose related:	Sedation, dizziness, ataxia
Hypersensitivity:	None reported
Chronic toxicity:	None reported
Teratogenic:	Unknown
Advantages:	Effective with low (dose related) side effect profile (no evidence of psychosis problems yet)
Disadvantages:	Thrice daily dosage (if necessary) is a slight problem, but may be needed to avoid dose dependent side effects

Topiramate

Trade name:	Topamax
Mode(s) of action:	Modulation of Na^+ x Ca^{++} conductance, enhancement of GABA activity, inhibition of Kainate mediated conductance. Weak carbonic anhydrase inhibitor. (Polytherapy in a single compound!)
Indications:	Add on therapy for resistant partial seizures with or without secondary generalization, trials in primary generalized epilepsy are taking place
Dose:	Go 'low and slow', 25 mg daily for 2 weeks, then increments of 25 mg (twice daily regimen) every 2 weeks until side effects prevent further increase, seizures stop or a total daily dose of 600 mg is reached. This drug probably has a flat dose response curve
'Therapeutic range':	Not measured
Side effects, dose related:	Sedative, slowed cognition, other neurotoxic symptoms, severe weight loss, psychosis/depression, peripheral tingling
Hypersensitivity:	None reported
Chronic toxicity:	Renal stones (avoid drug in those known to be predisposed) and ensure good fluid intake in all patients
Teratogenic:	Almost certainly. Women of childbearing potential should take folic acid (5 mg daily) while taking this drug (although this may not be protective).
Advantages:	Powerful and effective

Disadvantages:	Side effects are also powerful: cognitive impairment may clear eventually, but use of the drug is limited by side effects. Monitor patient's mental state carefully as depression and psychosis are of insidious onset

Note: Problems with psychosis/depression are not widely known but are reported from audited experience with this drug

Vigabatrin

Trade name:	Sabril
Mode(s) of action:	Enzyme activated suicidal inhibitor of GABA amino transferase (thus increasing GABA levels in the synaptic space)
Indications:	Add on for partial seizures with or without secondary generalization. Niche role in paediatrics (drug of choice in West syndrome). Not licensed (yet) for first line as trials in progress and not effective in primary generalized epilepsy (may make myoclonic jerks worse)
Dose:	Go low and slow: 500 mg daily for 2 weeks then increments of 500 mg every 2–4 weeks (once, twice daily dosage) to maximum of 3 g total daily dose
'Therapeutic range':	Not tested
Side effects, dose related:	Sedation (sometimes), weight gain, psychosis (probably mixed affective) depression, reduces phenytoin levels by 20% (reason unknown)
Hypersensitivity:	Nil reported
Chronic toxicity:*	**Recent reports of severe loss of peripheral vision in some patients taking this drug for more than 2 years give rise for concern**
Teratogenic:	Possibly (some animal data suggest this). Women of childbearing potential should take folic acid (5 mg daily) while taking this drug (although this may not be protective)

Cont'd.

Advantages:	Effective and very few interactions so easy to add on
Disadvantages:	Careful dose escalation usually avoids psychosis (its reputation for causing this was due to too rapid escalation). Has reputation for loss of efficacy over time (justified?): peripheral visual loss (if confirmed and shown to be common) will make it difficult to use except as a last resort

* Suggest do not initiate new prescribing of this drug until this question has been settled. It may prove advisable to withdraw this drug in patients who are not clearly benefitting from it and to screen, carefully, those who need to continue to take it for peripheral visual loss

Treatment issues in patients with learning difficulty and epilepsy

Primum non nocere

It is important to control seizures as completely as possible in people with learning difficulty since in some ways they are even more disabling than in people with normal learning capability. However medication is being given to a brain with already compromised cognitive function and in which there may be different neurochemical responses and mechanisms, an imbalance of homeostatic mechanisms and disruption to the relationship between inhibitory and excitatory mechanisms. People who have pre-existing learning difficulty are naturally more vulnerable to cognitive impairment induced by medication (although, rarely, inhibiting epileptic activity may improve their cognition).

For this reason, prescribing for people with learning difficulty involves walking a thin tightrope between control of seizures and over sedation and cognitive impairment. In some patients it may be necessary to try to control damaging subictal activity which is further impairing cognitive function, in other patients you may need to accept a limited objective of controlling the more damaging seizures (such as drop attacks). It would be important to choose medication which is as least sedating as possible, to use the minimum dosage to obtain control and to try to achieve monotherapy wherever possible.

In patients with dysfunctional brains paradoxical responses to medication may occur, behaviour changes may well be iatrogenic. It would also be best to choose, as far as possible, a broad spectrum anticonvulsant, as much epilepsy in patients with learning difficulty is multifocal secondary generalized (although primary generalized seizures do occur) **(Table 21)**.

Whichever drug is chosen it would be important to initiate treatment with a low dose and to escalate the dose slowly and carefully, giving enough time to estimate whether the drug at the present dose level has actually been effective before increasing the dose (monitoring changes in behaviour carefully). Changes in behaviour may be *negative* (development of irritability, aggressiveness, paranoid ideation) or *positive* (awakening, alerting, becoming more in contact with surroundings). Positive changes in behaviour may however be misinterpreted and the patient who 'wakes up' and becomes more demanding of carers may be labelled as having a behaviour disturbance when in fact the change in behaviour is actually an improvement.

Further reading

Rapeport W (1995) Factors influencing the relationship between carbamazepine, plasma concentration and its clinical effects in patients with epilepsy. *Clin Neuropharmacol* **8**: 141–149.

Shorvon S (1995) The drug treatment of epilepsy. In: *Epilepsy* (eds Hopkins A, Shorvon S, Cascino G), 2nd edn, pp.171–214. London: Chapman & Hall Medical.

Table 21
Anticonvulsant drugs and learning difficulty.

With all drugs start low, go slow	
Therapeutic windows are particularly likely to occur in the learning disabled	
Drugs recommended:	lamotrigine, gabapentin
Drugs to be used cautiously:	carbamazepine, sodium valproate, tiagabine, clobazam (intermittently)
Drugs to be avoided or used extremely cautiously:	vigabatrin, phenytoin, phenobarbitone, clonazapam and topiramate

Counselling and social support for people with epilepsy

As mentioned earlier the handicaps of epilepsy are social and psychological and their management is at least as important as the medical management of seizures, although often neglected. The physician and his non medical professional colleagues need to help patients overcome stigma (perceived or actual) (a) to overcome their fear of having seizures, (b) to prevent the person from becoming overprotected by well meaning relatives, (c) to minimize the cognitive impairments of epilepsy, (d) to help patients regain the feeling of control over their life and (e) to improve their quality of life. Episodes of depression are common with people with epilepsy (with a multifactorial cause): anxiety and stress undoubtedly make epilepsy worse. **Table 22** indicates a counselling checklist for people with newly acquired epilepsy, or for their carers.

Although attitudes are slowly changing epilepsy is still very much a stigmatized condition with both felt and perceived stigma. People who acquire epilepsy acquire a capacity to frighten and disturb other people and also take into the acquisition of their epilepsy the myths that they already have

Table 22
Birmingham Brainwave information and counselling checklist.

---

1. The nature of epilepsy
2. The reason for the patient's epilepsy
3. Appropriate genetic information
4. Discussion of treatment decisions
5. Appropriate information about drug interactions
6. Results of investigations and their interpretation
7. Appropriate first aid
8. Appropriate risk management (individualized)
9. Information about sport and swimming
10. Discussion about social implications of epilepsy
11. Discussion about self-control measures for epilepsy
12. Alcohol and epilepsy
13. Appropriate information and empowerment related to education
14. Appropriate information and empowerment related to employment
15. Appropriate information related to contraception and sexuality*
16. Appropriate information related to pregnancy*
17. Full information about driving*

* Record in the notes that this information has been given

---

about the condition, acquired from cultural beliefs (this is why newly acquired epilepsy in older people can be so emotionally and psychologically damaging).

People who acquire epilepsy, and their families, go through a period of stress, also seen in other disabling conditions, but particularly and sharply felt in epilepsy. There may be long periods of **denial**, prolonged periods of **sadness, grief** or **anger. Fear of the condition**, which may be very long lasting, is very likely to lead to **overprotection**. The child or adolescent with epilepsy is unnecessarily denied opportunities for recreation, work, social and sexual contact. It is important that children or adolescents with epilepsy are allowed and encouraged to do everything that other children and adolescents do, particularly such things as **bicycle riding, swimming, tree climbing, which tend to be automatically banned**. Overprotection is the most damaging form of handicap that people with epilepsy encounter, it is therefore important that both the patient and, if necessary, the family are encouraged to discuss the realistic risks of epilepsy to the individual so that sensible regimens and precautions and first aid can be worked out for the individual. Armed with sufficient information patients can take part in treatment decisions, understand the reason for their epilepsy (if it is known) and can be an advocate for themselves at school or at work and can be encouraged to have a full social and sexual life and, except in very unusual circumstances, be encouraged to drink alcohol socially.

Although every clinic that manages people with epilepsy should have access to good counselling services so the emotional responses to epilepsy can be worked through and the patient receive the necessary education, the doctor, himself or herself, should encourage self advocacy in the patient but should also be prepared to be a professional support, and an advocate in terms of ensuring that silly restrictions are not placed upon the patient in the workplace, at school or at college. The physician's role is also to monitor the patient's mental state carefully. Most people with epilepsy are helped by contact with the British Epilepsy Association and its support groups (or the equivalent organizations in Ireland and Scotland). There are some support groups, however, that can be unhelpful if they encourage dependency and negative stereotypes.

Surgical treatment for epilepsy

Increasingly surgery is an option to be considered for patients with partial onset epilepsy which does not come under satisfactory control with anticonvulsant medication. In many patients (e.g. with partial seizures related to mesial temporal sclerosis) surgery, if it is to be successful, should be considered early on (if the patient has not got control with medication after 2 years) rather than waiting for many years before surgery is thought of. The majority of surgery in this country is carried out for patients with intractable partial seizures related to unilateral temporal lobe epilepsy (in patients usually with identifiable unilateral mesial temporal sclerosis). Results of surgery in this group are very impressive. Surgery can also be carried out on partial seizures with frontal onset (because success is less than in temporal lobe surgery, surgeons will usually only attempt it if there is a clear resectable structural lesion in the frontal lobe which accounts for the epilepsy).

Patients being assessed for surgery need full investigation including high quality MRI scanning, ictal EEG recording (in 20% of patients, with some kind of invasive electrode procedure) and neuropsychological testing to ensure that resection of the piece of the brain under consideration will not lead to severe memory or speech problems. Neuropsychological testing includes (at the moment) the **carotid amytal** or **WADA test** which involves temporarily anaesthetizing one half of the brain whilst testing memory and speech function in the unaffected half. In some patients functional imaging of the brain (SPECT, PET) may also be helpful; some centres use magneto encephalography and MRI spectroscopy to pinpoint resectable lesions in the brain. Surgery for epilepsy should only be carried out in a centre with a surgeon who is experienced in epilepsy surgery.

Most epilepsy surgery now (excluding resective surgery for tumours, AVMs, etc.) is as minimal as possible, but other operations are available in selected cases.

Subpial resection

In areas of the brain, particularly the motor cortex (where resection would be impossible without causing too much damage to the patient), multiple cuts can be made in the motor cortex which does not affect motor function (or sensory function) but does reduce or stop seizure propagation.

Corpus callosotomy

In patients with severe drop attacks which cannot be controlled medically sectioning the anterior two thirds of the corpus collosum can sometimes reduce the frequency of such attacks considerably or even abolish them.

Hemispherectomy

In patients disabled by infantile hemiplegia with severe unilateral (sometimes secondary generalized) motor seizures arising in the damaged cortex, if medical treatment fails then resection of the damaged cortex can be attempted which often relieves the epilepsy without making the hemiplegia any worse. This is a specialized operation in which care has to be exercised to avoid long term side effects, but it can be extremely helpful. It is best attempted reasonably early on before secondary epileptogenesis occurs in the normal cortex.

Vagal stimulation

There is evidence that electrical stimulation of the left vagal nerve in the neck by means of an implanted stimulator (which automatically stimulates the vagal nerve for a defined period every hour and can also be activated by the patient using an external magnet) can be successful in controlling seizures in otherwise intractable epilepsy. This is a relatively new treatment which is just beginning to be used in the UK but there is some control trial evidence to suggest that it is effective in some patients. It may, after further evaluation, turn out to have a particular use in patients with learning difficulty and severe epilepsy, but this remains to be established.

Epilepsy surgery in people with mental illness or learning difficulty

Most surgical authorities regard mental illness and learning difficulty (IQ under 70) as relative contraindications to epilepsy surgery. If a patient has both epilepsy and a psychiatric illness and would be otherwise suitable for surgery, it should be appreciated that even if the surgery is successful in terms of controlling seizures, it is very unlikely to have any effect on the psychiatric illness. Likewise most epilepsy in people with learning difficulty is multifocal and even if it is not, resective surgery is likely to lead to even further reduction in intelligence and learning ability. However, these rules are not absolute and occasionally it may be helpful in the rehabilitation of people with epilepsy and psychiatric disorder for patients to lose their seizures as part of their rehabilitation. An operation such as a hemispherectomy or corpus callosotomy and occasionally resective surgery can sometimes be justified in people with learning difficulty. In both situations, however, informed consent for surgery may be difficult to obtain.

Psychiatric and psychological reactions after surgery

Depressive illnesses, occasionally schizophreniform psychoses, anxiety and adjustment reactions are not uncommon after successful resective surgery for epilepsy, although most are transient. Suddenly losing seizures (with all the psychological and social adjustments that are occasioned by such a dramatic life change) is bound to produce adjustment reactions in some individuals. The question is whether or not they can be predicted and whether, indeed, they matter (since most can be supported through and will get better). Some surgeons advocate presurgical psychiatric screening, rejecting for surgery those patients who appear to be predisposed to postoperative psychiatric illness. In the current state of knowledge this is probably a mistake, partly because predictive reliability is probably low and because most postoperative psychological reactions can be worked through and treated. Preoperative psychiatric screening should perhaps be used to identify those patients who will need psychological support after surgery rather than to reject patients for surgery.

Further reading

Engel J (1994) Epilepsy surgery. *Curr Opin Neurol Neurosurg* 7:140–147.

Engel J (ed) (1993) *Surgical Treatment of the Epilepsies*. New York: Raven Press.

Other non-medical treatments for epilepsy

Ketogenic diet

Occasionally intractable epilepsies in children, particularly the Lennox–Gastaut syndrome, respond to a diet which supplies the majority of dietary calories as fat. The child undergoes a couple of days of starvation until it becomes ketotic and then medium-chain triglycerides are introduced into the diet, the rest of the diet being carefully supervised. This treatment can be successful but requires careful dietary supervision for success.

Psychological treatment of epilepsy

Apart from the necessary psychological support that all people with epilepsy need if they are to come to terms with the diagnosis, specific psychological therapies can have an important part to play in the management of some epilepsies, although often unnecessarily relegated to last resort treatments. There is some evidence that if applied early they may be particularly effective.[34]

The general principles of the psychological treatment of epilepsy are based on several premises: that some seizures are triggered off by stress or anxiety so that stress management may have an important part to play in treating some epilepsies,[35] that some seizures are arousal mediated,[2] that seizure activity can be conditioned and be reinforced and that the reflex epilepsies are often best managed psychologically.[7] There is also evidence that many (perhaps 30%) of people with epilepsy can recognize reliable warnings that a seizure is coming and apply some kind of control technique.[36]

Stress and epilepsy

Epilepsy may briefly change the way a person thinks, feels, and acts — but how someone thinks, feels and acts may also change his or her epilepsy. Epilepsy takes place in a brain that also contains a mind, which is subject to other influences, both internal and external, and has differing states of arousal and emotion. They may have their own influences on the epilepsy.[35] There is both clinical and laboratory evidence to suggest that stress increases seizure frequency. This is something which many patients will report to their doctors (if asked) but has also been shown to be true in field studies with carefully collected data and in laboratory studies of EEG activation. 'Stress' usually increases seizure frequency but occasionally has the reverse effect, seizures being more frequent as stress levels fall. Apart from the direct effect of stress other stress factors which may be important in the genesis of seizures are **involuntary hyperventilation, poor sleep patterns induced by anxiety, low morale leading to poor compliance with medication and overindulgence in alcohol.** There is evidence that specific mood states such as guilt may also precipitate seizures.[36] Hyperventilation and sleep deprivation are, of course, specific measures used for the activation of seizures and abnormal activity in the EEG.

Reflex epilepsy

The best example of the reflex epilepsies is photosensitive/pattern sensitive epilepsy. In this type of reflex epilepsy absence, myoclonic or tonic clonic seizures are induced by flickering light of the right intensity and frequency, or by specific visual patterns. This form of reflux epilepsy has been particularly studied since the advent of the domestic television set has made it clinically important. It appears to be a purely biological phenomenon which has its roots in some animal epilepsies.[37]

It is important to recognize those patients with primary generalized epilepsy who are flicker or pattern sensitive, since they may have induced seizures in front of television monitors or computer screens (some computer induced epilepsy is related to pattern sensitivity). Although photo and pattern sensitivity can often be controlled by appropriate medication (sodium valproate and probably lamotrigine), if patients know they are liable to have seizures if exposed to flickering light or to a particular type of pattern, simple behavioural precautions can also be helpful. People who are photosensitive to a range of flicker which includes that of a domestic television set should sit at least 8 feet away from it, have the light behind it, and cover one eye if they have to approach the set closer (most photosensitive epilepsy needs binocular stimulation to induce a seizure).

Other reflex epilepsies

Most of the other recognized reflex epilepsies have a strong psychological component and can often be managed psychologically. Reflex epilepsies occur when the patient is exposed to a specific stimulus which reliably triggers off a seizure. In musicogenic epilepsy, for instance, the seizure is induced by a particular tune (rather than by music at a particular pitch). In voice induced epilepsy it is a particular voice that triggers off the seizure; in language induced epilepsy it is a particular phrase (rather than just hearing somebody speaking); in touch induced epilepsy, the inducing touch is usually on a particular part of the body. In many patients with reflex epilepsies there is a clear emotional association to their stimulus: for many patients just *thinking* about the inducing stimulus is enough to trigger off a seizure. In one man, for instance, with touch induced epilepsy of the face (which was usually induced by shaving), merely thinking about shaving would induce abnormal epileptic activity in the EEG. Some reflex triggers are very specific (e.g. in one patient, contemplating a closed safety pin was perfectly safe, but contemplating an open safety pin immediately induced a seizure). Most reflex epilepsies are probably induced by an emotional association with the stimulus and sometimes relate to circumstances occurring at the time of the first seizure (e.g. in one patient with musicogenic epilepsy the particular tune to which she was sensitive had been playing at the time she had her first seizure).

REFLEX EPILEPSIES

- Flicker induced
- Complex pattern induced epilepsy
- Reading induced epilepsy
- Startle induced epilepsy
- Musicogenic epilepsy
- Voice induced epilepsy
- Language induced epilepsy
- Touch and vibration induced epilepsy
- Eating induced epilepsy
- Taste (of food) induced epilepsy
- Immersion (hot or cold water) induced epilepsy
- Sexual stimulation induced epilepsy
- Arithmetical calculation induced epilepsy
- Strategic thinking (e.g. chess induced) epilepsy

Specific emotional feelings (guilt, sadness, etc.) can also act as precipitants of reflex epilepsy. Although most patients learn to avoid the stimulus which triggers off a reflex seizure they are sometimes unable to. They sometimes welcome it: **self induced epilepsy** is often produced by some kind of reflex mechanism and it is clear that the patient who indulges in inducing epilepsy obtains

some kind of satisfaction from it — this is particularly true of flicker induced epilepsy in children, who learn to do it by flickering their hand between their eyes and the sun.

Psychological techniques that have been used in managing epilepsy

Reflex epilepsies are often managed by massed practice,[38] and once the response has been extinguished with continuous stimulation, providing the patient practises the stimulation on a daily basis, seizures often do remain extinguished.

In assessing the results of the behavioural or psychological technique for managing epilepsy there are obviously strong placebo factors and although behavioural techniques are quite widely used properly controlled trials involving placebo treatment have rarely been employed.[39] Many studies in the literature have been single patient studies in some of which it has not been possible to be certain that it was epilepsy that was being treated.[36,40] However there is sufficient evidence to suggest that certain psychological techniques are effective in the management of some epileptic seizures. Rewarding seizure free periods and 'punishing' seizure activity has been shown (against controls) to be effective in children's epilepsy, as has specific relaxation therapy aimed at seizure reduction.[39]

TECHNIQUES THAT HAVE BEEN SHOWN TO BE EFFECTIVE IN CONTROLLING EPILEPTIC SEIZURES

- *Operant conditioning*
- *Anxiety management*
- *Cue controlled arousal manipulation*
- *Countermeasures*

Learning specific relaxation cues that alter arousal quickly has also been shown to be effective and some patients can develop effective countermeasures, e.g. rubbing the part of the body in which a sensory aura is developing, or gripping the hand in which a motor seizure is starting or using an effort of will or concentration. Many people with epilepsy try their own 'homemade' control measures (usually trying to increase arousal). There is some evidence that they might better try to reduce arousal.[7,41,42]

Alternative therapies

Many people with epilepsy, dissatisfied with the side effects of medication and the sometimes dismissive attitudes of doctors, are turning to the alternative therapies. There is little evidence as to their effectiveness, but most will do no harm: anything that reduces stress and gives the patient a feeling of control is probably going to be helpful and should not be discouraged. What should be discouraged are alternative therapists over enthusiastic about the effectiveness of their particular technique who urge patients to throw their medicines away. This particularly applies to those who offer religious conversion as a cure for epilepsy. Some alternative therapies can be used in conjunction with behavioural methods, as in the 'smell memory' technique.[43]

Further reading

Betts T (1993) Neuropsychiatry. In: *A Textbook of Epilepsy* (eds J Laidlaw, A Richens and D Chadwick), 4th edn, pp.443–48. Edinburgh: Churchill Livingstone.

Forster F (1997) Reflex Epilepsy. In: *Behaviour Therapy and Conditional Reflexes*. Springfield: Charles C Thomas.

Lockard J (1980) A primate model of clinical epilepsy: mechanisms of action through quantifications of therapeutic effects. In: *Epilepsy: A Window to Brain Mechanisms* (eds J Lockard and A Ward). New York: Raven Press.

Schwartz R, Eaton J, Bower B and Aynsley-Green A (1989) Ketogenic diets in the treatment of epilepsy; short term clinical effects. *Dev Med Child Neurol* **31**: 145–51.

Women with epilepsy

13

The effect of epilepsy (both physically and psychologically) and its treatment on the sexual and reproductive life of women (and their offspring) has now become a focus of speculation and research. There is a growing corpus of knowledge which should guide physicians' behaviour, although clinics for gender related problems in epilepsy are still rare.

The menstrual cycle and epilepsy

There is evidence that the phases of the menstrual cycle can have an effect on the frequency of epileptic seizures, with peak seizure frequency occurring at ovulation or immediately prior to menstruation and during it. Epilepsy itself can have an effect on the regularity of the menstrual cycle. In one recent study, for instance, it was shown that 35% of women with epilepsy had anovulatory cycles compared with only 8% of controls. This effect seemed to be mainly in women with partial seizures compared to primary generalized seizures.[44]

Compared to women without epilepsy there is a marked increase in the incidence of the polycystic ovary syndrome (characterized by raised testosterone levels, anovulatory cycles, polycystic ovaries, hirsutism, menstrual irregularity and often obesity) in women with epilepsy.[45] This menstrual irregularity including the polycystic ovary syndrome (which has a potential threat to fertility) may be the result of the epilepsy itself interfering with the release of gonadotropins in the mid-brain with an increase in luteinizing hormone pulse frequency.

The polycystic ovary syndrome has been particularly associated with sodium valproate (Epilim). It has been suggested that enzyme inducing antiepileptic drugs (such as phenytoin and carbamazepine), by effectively reducing testosterone levels may actually prevent the development of this syndrome.[45] If this is the case the newer non enzyme inducing anti-epileptic drugs, such as lamotrigine and gabapentin, may also, when used in monotherapy, appear to have a spurious association with the polycystic ovary syndrome, although there is no evidence for this: indeed, what evidence there is suggests these drugs

have no effect on ovarian function. Most authors continue to believe that sodium valproate may have a causative role in the polycystic ovary syndrome particularly because of its apparent association with obesity and hyperinsulinism.

Seizure frequency changes during the normal menstrual cycle are presumably related to changing sex hormone concentrations during the menstrual cycle. It is generally considered that oestrogen is epileptogenic and progesterone has some anticonvulsant properties. It is likely that seizure frequency increases at times in the menstrual cycle when oestrogen levels are at their highest. Other factors may be important such as changes in anticonvulsant levels during the menstrual cycle and the mood changes that take place in some women during the cycle: water retention may also play a part.

Hormone manipulation, particularly progesterone therapy and anti-oestrogen drugs, have been suggested for women whose seizures consistently cluster premenstrually, although firm evidence for their effectiveness is lacking. Anticonvulsant drug doses can be increased perimenstrually or short courses of acetazolamide or clobazam given at the point of greatest seizure risk, if the woman's menstrual cycle can be accurately timed. Occasionally suppression of menstruation with depot progesterones may also be effective.

Fertility

There is a small but significant reduction in fertility in women with epilepsy, although this possible biological effect is compounded by other factors, particularly social ones and the fact that people with learning difficulty or other handicaps (which will include women with severe epilepsies) also have low fertility rates. A population study suggests that fertility in women with epilepsy was initially very low but has been rising over the decades,[46] although it still may be lower than in the general female population.[47]

Contraception

It is now generally recognized that enzyme inducing antiepileptic drugs (phenobarbitone, mysoline, phenytoin, carbamazepine and, possibly, topiramate) are associated with contraceptive failure when conventional dose combined oral contraceptives are used. Enzyme induction increases the breakdown of oestrogen (and possibly progesterone) in such pills. Sadly there is evidence that this is in fact little known to neurologists or obstetricians who continue to report contraceptive failures among their patients taking antiepileptic drugs.[48]

Women taking an enzyme inducing anticonvulsant should take at least 50 μg of ethinyl oestradiol in their pill, if breakthrough bleeding occurs the dose may have to be increased to 75 μg or even 100 μg. It is possible that even with a higher oestrogen dose full contraceptive efficacy is still absent. Patients taking lamotrigine, gabapentin, vigabatrin, sodium valproate or a benzodiazepine without an enzyme inducing agent can use a normal dose oral contraceptive.

There is little agreement about whether such enzyme inducing drugs significantly affect progesterone only pills (the mini pill). Certainly in our clinic at the moment we consider their efficacy not to be affected but suggest that in women taking depot progesterones (such as Depo-Provera, which in many ways is a suitable contraceptive for women with epilepsy) the frequency of injections is every 10 weeks rather than every 12. Implants of levonorgestrel ('Norplant') however cannot be recommended as contraceptive failures have been regularly reported in women taking enzyme inducing drugs with this particular device. Further work needs to be done in this area as progesterone only contraception increases in popularity. For full reliability with combined oral contraceptives in women taking enzyme inducing drugs an additional barrier or spermicidal method should be used as well; it is imperative that women are informed of the extra risk. In our clinic, women with frequent seizures which may lead to forgetfulness are advised to use a method of contraception which does not rely on memory for its efficacy. There is no reason why women with epilepsy should not use the coil; in my experience there is a slight risk of a seizure induced when the neck of the womb is stretched, so intravenous diazepam and resuscitation equipment should be available.

Sexuality

There is long standing and reasonably compelling evidence that women with epilepsy have diminished sexual lives compared with their peer group. This seems to be a disorder of sexual arousal rather than sexual desire and is independent of seizure frequency, seizure type, anticonvulsant medication, mood disorder or the time that seizures first appeared. Many of these disorders are treatable. Our own experience suggests that although possibly in some women endocrine and other causes may be implicated in the sexual disorder in many it is fear of a seizure during the sexual act which inhibits sexuality. For a full review see Morrell and Guldner.[49]

Pregnancy and epilepsy

Three excellent reviews have recently been published which should be consulted for a full discussion of the available literature.[50–52] What follows is the present operating policy of the preconception clinic of Birmingham Brainwave relating to the management of the women with epilepsy before and after conception. **The majority of women with epilepsy have uncomplicated pregnancies and normal offspring.**

1. Women with epilepsy are more prone to potentially serious complications of pregnancy including antepartum haemorrhage, spontaneous abortion, premature rupture of the membranes, premature

birth, low birth weight infants and neonatal death. This may be a consequence of medication or may be a consequence of fetal hypoxia and acidosis caused by maternal seizures. The majority of women with epilepsy should be delivered in hospital, be closely monitored before delivery and treated as a special risk group (as are mothers with diabetes). They should also have access to clinical genetic services and preconception counselling.

2. There is an increased risk of fetal abnormality in all women with epilepsy, irrespective of whether or not they are having seizures, or whether or not they are taking anticonvulsant medication. Even in women who are seizure free and not taking medication, the fetal abnormality rate is probably about 1% above that of the general population. Its aetiology is obscure and may be related to genetic factors associated with the epilepsy. Men with epilepsy, however, do not seem to influence fetal outcome in their offspring whether or not they are still having seizures or whether or not they are taking medication.

3. The fetal abnormality rate increases if the woman's seizures are controlled but she is taking anticonvulsant medication, it increases further if she is having convulsive seizures. The risk of fetal damage depends on what anticonvulsant medication is taken and increases if the woman is taking more than one anticonvulsant. Convulsive seizures in late pregnancy are associated with increased risk to the mother (particularly from inhalation of gastric contents during the seizure) and probably to the fetus (from injury sustained in falling or from fetal anoxia or acidosis).

4. Fetal damage is particularly likely to occur in women taking phenytoin or sodium valproate and has also been described with phenobarbitone, primidone and carbamazepine. The potential effects of these anticonvulsants on the fetus are fairly similar except that sodium valproate (and possibly carbamazepine) is associated with neural tube defects (spina bifida). The majority of reported abnormalities are however oral, facial, cardiovascular and digital malformations, particularly cleft lip and palate and ventricular septal defects. Hypospadias in male infants has also been described; minor morphological abnormalities are also common in children born to women taking anticonvulsants includ-

ing hypertelorism, epicanthal folds, abnormalities of the nose and philtrum and nail hypoplasia.

5. Mechanisms that produce these abnormalities are multiple including possible genetic susceptibility brought out by the anticonvulsant, the effect of free radical metabolites of anticonvulsants or the accumulation of toxic drug intermediates, and folic acid deficiency induced by anticonvulsant medication. It is possible that drugs that are enzyme inducing may be particularly likely to cause birth defects (although benzodiazepine fetal abnormalities have also been described).

6. Low folic acid levels are known to be implicated in fetal abnormality and all women are recommended, before becoming pregnant, to be taking sufficient folic acid to prevent neural tube defects. Phenytoin, carbamazepine and barbiturates cause folic acid malabsorption and sodium valproate is known to interfere with folic acid metabolism.

7. Animal studies of teratogenesis have shown that all the older anticonvulsants produce fetal abnormalities in the offspring of animals exposed to the anticon-

vulsant in utero. This does not seem to be the case with some of the newer anticonvulsants, particularly lamotrigine and gabapentin,[52] but there is not yet sufficient clinical experience with these two drugs to be completely certain that they do not have teratogenic effects in humankind, although evidence is slowly accumulating that they do not.

Various recommendations can therefore be suggested for the woman with epilepsy who wishes to become pregnant and for whom preconception counselling would seem to be particularly important.

1. Before conception a joint decision should be made by the woman and her physician, if she is completely controlled, whether it would be safe for her to withdraw from her medication before attempting conception. The withdrawal criteria established by the Medical Research Council drug withdrawal study would suggest that many women who have been seizure free for at least 5 years could safely slowly withdraw from their medication and remain seizure free (although there are some forms of epilepsy such as juvenile myoclonic epilepsy where withdrawal would be inadvisable).

2. If withdrawal is not possible (sometimes a temporary withdrawal can be achieved whilst a woman becomes pregnant; she can start retaking anticonvulsants after the third month of pregnancy) then wherever possible medication should be rationalized to one of the safer anticonvulsants. In our own clinic we feel that lamotrigine is now to be recommended as the safest drug for a woman to take if she wishes to become pregnant and it is our policy to substitute lamotrigine, wherever possible, for valproate and phenytoin — although not all authorities agree with this. Our decision about lamotrigine is based on its clean animal teratogenicity data.

3. If there are good reasons for continuing an anticonvulsant which is known to carry particular risk then efforts should be made to ensure that the drug is within the therapeutic range on serum level testing; if valproate is the chosen drug it should be given three or four times a day to avoid sudden peaks in blood level. Certain drug combinations, such as phenytoin plus sodium valproate, should be avoided.

4. All women with epilepsy, whether it is still active or not and whether or not they are still taking anticonvulsants should (from well before conception and throughout the pregnancy) take 5 mg of folic acid daily. This is an arbitrary dose but is safe and very unlikely to make epilepsy worse.

5. Pregnancy has a variable effect on seizure frequency (it usually has little effect), although in later pregnancy because of changes in absorption kinetics of most drugs, blood levels of the patient's anticonvulsant may fall — serum drug levels of some drugs may need to be monitored and doses increased in the latter stages of pregnancy to maintain seizure control.

6. Close cooperation between the doctor managing the woman's epilepsy and the doctor managing the pregnancy should be established. It is our own recommendation that in labour itself exhaustion should be avoided as should hyperventilation in the second stage, pain control should avoid the use of pethidine if possible. Audit has shown that epidural anaesthesia is safe for women with epilepsy, although often denied to them.

7. Breast feeding is safe, even if the woman is taking anticonvulsants (her child, after all, has been exposed to the anticonvulsant for

9 months in the womb) and should be encouraged to aid bonding between mother and child.

8. Post partum, individual counselling and help should be offered to the mother (particularly if she is a single mother) so that she can, even if she continues to have seizures, bring up her child safely, by adopting and utilizing simple precautions.

Epilepsy and the menopause

Very little work has been done in this area and there are several problems that have not yet been resolved. On theoretical grounds women with epilepsy taking anticonvulsants, particularly the older anticonvulsants which have some effect on calcium metabolism,

should, when approaching the menopause, be considered for hormone replacement therapy. Clinical experience suggests that this is difficult to achieve; hormone replacement therapy in many women with epilepsy at the menopause often seems to increase seizure frequency. Most women, particularly those with premenstrual exacerbation to their seizures, can look forward to some diminution in their seizure frequency (if not already controlled) at the menopause. A small number of women, for reasons totally unknown, seem to start epilepsy at the menopause; this whole area needs thorough investigation.

Further reading

Tomson T, Gram L, Sillanpää M and Johannessen S (eds) (1997) *Epilepsy and Pregnancy.* Petersfield: Wrightson Biomedical Publishing.

Intelligence, learning, cognition and epilepsy

There is no evidence to suggest that there is a *direct* link between epilepsy and intelligence. Epilepsy can be found in those with the highest intelligence and intellectual achievement (indeed its prevalence in university students is the same as in the general population). But there is an *indirect* association between epilepsy and intelligence in that the more severe a person's mental retardation the more likely that person is to also have epilepsy, partly because the condition that causes the retardation also causes the epilepsy and partly because the more severely the brain is damaged the more likely it is to have epilepsy. In the profoundly mentally retarded nearly 50% will also have epilepsy; in those with only mild retardation about 5% will have epilepsy in addition. For a description of those conditions that cause both learning impairment and epilepsy see the section on aetiology and also Kirkham.[53] Most of these present in childhood and are, at least initially, managed by paediatric neurologists but will eventually come under the care of the psychiatrist specializing in learning difficulty, who must, therefore, have an excellent knowledge of the scope, and limitations, of the management of epilepsy in this population.

In the learning impaired with epilepsy several problems related to diagnosis, treatment and associated behavioural problems stand out. There is no doubt that epilepsy is overdiagnosed in people with learning difficulty, partly because other neurological phenomena like dystonias are common in the learning disabled, partly because of lack of subjective verbal description and partly because acting out behaviour is particularly likely to be paroxysmal and thus mistaken for epilepsy (see the section on Investigation). Anticonvulsants can have paradoxical and unexpected effects in the learning disabled and may in this population be particularly likely to have a 'therapeutic window' (see the section on Management). Finally certain behavioural characteristics of the learning impaired may be particularly common in those with epilepsy, e.g. *autism, hyperactivity* and *self injurious behaviour*, and may be sometimes exacerbated by anticonvulsant drugs.

But even in patients without obvious learning difficulty cognitive impairment can occur in several modalities **(Table 23)** and is multifactorial in its aetiology. It should also be remembered that epilepsy can have effects on neuronal transmitter and receptor function far beyond its apparent area of localization (see the section on Basic mechanisms) and has effects on mood and motivation which may also impair learning and cognitive func-

tion; impairment may be specific to a particular aspect of cognition or learning or be more generalized **(Table 24)**.

Seizure activity can obviously interrupt the mechanisms of memory and learning: much of this activity is subictal, not clinically obvious but still present. Even when such activity is absent epilepsy associated neuronal dysfunction will still be present. Focal activity or dysfunction can be impairing, even if only in a small area, if that area is critical to a specific function (e.g. the hippocampus) or if damage or activity is bilateral (e.g. in schizencephaly). Focal impairment is more likely to be damaging if it is in the left hemisphere rather than the right. Generalized damage or dysfunction becomes impairing once it has passed Lashley's critical mass; further slight decrement in neuronal mass or function leads to disproportionate loss in cognitive function (this is why people with severe but static acquired brain damage can dement rapidly as they age). Anti-epileptic medication can have marked further impairment on cognitive function in already compromised brains (an effect not seen in people with normal brain function).

Further reading

Corbett J (1993) Epilepsy and mental handicap. In: *A Textbook of Epilepsy*, (eds J Laidlaw, A Richens and D Chadwick). 4th edn, Edinburgh: Churchill Livingstone, pp. 631–36.

Table 23
Modalities of cognitive function affected by epilepsy.[54]

Intellect/academic achievement

Including intelligence, reading comprehension, spelling, mathematical reasoning, numerical operations, listening comprehension, oral expression

Attention

Including sustained attention, selective attention, attentional capacity

Abstraction/mental flexibility

Including concept formation and sorting/set shifting

Visuo-spatial ability

Including construction, copying and matching

Learning/memory

Including primary, secondary and tertiary memory

Language

Receptive and expressive

Sensory/psychomotor skills

Including simple motor, complex motor, cognitive motor and sensory perceptual

---

Table 24
Possible causes of cognitive impairment in people with epilepsy.

1. Focal structural lesion, e.g. tumour, mesial temporal sclerosis
2. Generalized neuronal loss
3. Focal epileptic activity
4. Focal sub-ictal activity
5. Generalized epileptic activity
6. Generalized sub-ictal activity
7. Focal neuronal dysfunction
8. Generalized neuronal dysfunction
9. Impaired mood/motivation
10. Effect of anticonvulsant medication

Mental illness and epilepsy

Introduction

From the earliest recorded medical writing until the late nineteenth century epilepsy was usually considered a mental disorder and segregated and treated as such. This may have partly been due to the stigma and fear attached to this condition but also, no doubt, because uncontrolled epilepsy must have often produced profound mental impairment and delirium. In 1900 about 20% of an asylum's residents had epilepsy and psychiatrists had already recognized that 'moral treatment' was more important than intoxicating bromides and had described (but not recognized the significance of) the affective and psychotic disorders associated with epilepsy.[55] Epilepsy then separated from psychiatry and became the province of neurologists (to the detriment of both psychiatry and people with epilepsy!) and, in order to try to remove its stigma, epilepsy was 'sanitized' and interest in its psychiatric aspects lost, particularly with the development of effective drug treatment and the electroencephalogram. In the mid-twentieth century with the development of the concept of temporal lobe epilepsy the era of 'psychomotor peculiarity' was born and interest in the psychiatric illnesses associated with epilepsy rediscovered (although electroconvulsive therapy was developed out of a misunderstanding of the relationship between epilepsy and psychotic illness).

This interest has been maintained but the literature is confused and there is little agreement about the epidemiology, phenomenology or aetiology of the mental disorders of epilepsy. The reason for this is that different populations have been studied, different definitions and measurements of mental illness used and only rarely have comparisons with a control population been made. Because of the apparent association between temporal lobe epilepsy and psychiatric illness much effort has been spent on trying to show that mental illness is commoner in patients with left temporal epileptic foci. However, selected populations, unreliable methods of determining the side of an epileptic focus (unless an *ictal* recording, the EEG is unreliable — and even ictal foci may occur in patients with MRI or PET foci on the contralateral side!) and differing criteria for diagnosing mental illness have made comparison of various studies difficult and the matter remains unresolved (contrast the views of Trimble[56] and Stevens[57] for instance).

Epidemiology

Depending on the population studied, how selected it is, whether a control series is utilized and the definitions used, the prevalence of mental illness in people with epilepsy is probably greater than that expected by chance. For a review see Fenwick,[58] who suggests that in general population surveys perhaps 30–50% of people with epilepsy have some kind of measurable psychiatric morbidity (but often of a minor kind); it is not always apparent how many of the non-epileptic population would have similar morbidity. In clinic populations the percentage of patients with epilepsy with psychiatric morbidity is much higher.

Classification

Table 25 illustrates the traditional ictal related classification of mental disorder and epilepsy which has some validity, although most serious illness has no time relationship to the seizure itself (although it may have a relationship to changes in seizure frequency). Some patients have consistent changes in feeling or behaviour for some hours (sometimes days) before a seizure — so called *prodromal symptoms*. Prodromes do not seem to be related to epileptic discharge as such but probably relate to some putative metabolic

Table 25
Time relationship of the psychiatric syndrome to the seizure.

1. Peri-ictal

   a) Prodromal

   b) Aura

   c) Ictal (including partial status)

   d) Post-ictal

2. Inter-ictal

change prior to a seizure. They may trouble the patient, or be more of a problem to relatives if there are changes in mood or irritability, and may persist for a long time if seizures are otherwise successfully controlled (but usually eventually disappear under those circumstances). Depression, anxiety and hallucinatory experiences may occur regularly as an *aura* (a simple partial seizure) before a major seizure. If the major seizure is controlled they may become more prominent, frequent and troublesome.

Ictal depression, anxiety, hallucinatory experiences, aggression and episodes of amnesia, confusion and brief automatisms may occur as part of a simple or complex partial seizure. Stereotyped but prolonged behavioural changes may occur as part of *complex partial* (rarely *simple partial) status (twilight state)* and may take some time to recognize. *Sub-*

convulsive generalized status usually presents as a fluctuating confusional state. In any patient (with or without epilepsy) with recurrent stereotypical episodes of psychiatric symtomatology, particularly if accompanied by apparent confusion, an EEG obtained during the episodes is well worthwhile.

Post-ictal confusion, dysthymia and rarely severe depression are encountered as regularly occurring phenomena. Severe post-ictal aggression (epileptic furor) is now very uncommon. Recurrent post-ictal psychosis (often with a lucid interval between the end of the seizure and the onset of the psychosis) is a recognized phenomenon best described by Logsdail and Toone.[59]

All ictal related psychiatric symptoms are best treated by controlling the seizures.

Changes in ictal frequency and psychiatric symptoms

Changes in seizure frequency may be no more than random fluctuations; they do not imply that the amount of epileptic activity in the brain has actually changed but do seem to be sometimes associated with alterations in mental state. The concept (and even the translation) of Landolt's 'forced normalization' has been questioned[60] but clinical experience suggests that loss of seizure activity (particularly if sudden, whether or not it is spontaneous or induced by medication or surgery) is followed, more commonly than might be expected by chance, by a usually short-lived anxiety or depressive episode, rarely a psychosis. Sudden *increase* in seizure activity can be followed by hypomania or a confusional psychosis or brief delirium.[7]

Interictal mental symptoms

Aetiology

As with all mental symptoms aetiology of these epilepsy related psychiatric conditions is multifactorial, relating to brain damage (focal and generalized), on-going epileptic activity (focal and generalized), chronic receptor and transmitter dysfunction (focal and generalized), and social, psychological and genetic factors. Anticonvulsant medication may play a part (certain drugs, particularly *vigabatrin, ethosuximide* and possibly *topiramate,* are thought more likely to induce depression or psychosis than other drugs but not all authorities agree with this) and reduction of serum folate levels has also been suggested as an aetiological factor.

Personality disorder

The old belief in an 'epileptic personality' can no longer be justified and there is no personality type particularly associated with epilepsy.[61] The aberrant personality characteristics that are to be found in people with epilepsy are those often found in the brain damaged and socially and educationally stigmatized. Schwartz has introduced the useful concept of 'social apraxia' to describe the personality changes that occur in some people with epilepsy.[62] Although ictal rage can very rarely occur, there is no evidence that people with epilepsy are more aggressive.

Anxiety (Table 26)

Anxiety is a common (perhaps the commonest, if little studied) concomitant of epilepsy, not surprisingly as seizures can be so disturbing, both to the victim and to onlookers. Patients (and families) can develop anxiety

Table 26
Relationship between anxiety and epilepsy.[7]

1. Anxiety, generalized or phobic, related to fear of having a seizure
2. 'Post-traumatic' stress disorder related to threatening incident in seizure
3. Anxiety, generalized or phobic, related to family or social stigmatization of epilepsy.
4. Prodromal anxiety
5. Anxiety as an aura
6. Ictal anxiety (including 'twilight state')
7. Post-ictal anxiety disorder
8. Anxiety (usually expressed as agitation) as part of epilepsy related psychosis or organic brain disease
9. Anxiety that precipitates a seizure
10. Anxiety phenomena mistaken for epilepsy

about, and fear of, seizures and post-traumatic stress disorder (with ruminations, flashbacks, phobic avoidance, nightmares and hypervigilance) can occur if something life threatening (like a seizure in the bath) occurs during an attack. Anxiety can precipitate seizures (see the section on Psychological management) and be mistaken for them (see the section on Is it epilepsy?) Anxiety as an aura or ictal anxiety is comparatively common. The management of anxiety in people with epilepsy should be behavioural and cognitive, coupled with general counselling support. Medication should be avoided:

benzodiazepines because of their anticonvulsant effect (which will make withdrawal more than usually difficult) and antidepressants because of their seizure precipitating effect.

Affective illness

Depression (Table 27)

Affective disorder is far commoner in epilepsy that psychosis, is an important part of the management of epilepsy, but has always been neglected (even though suicide is an important cause of mortality in young

Table 27
Relationship between depression
and epilepsy.[7]

Depressive reaction ('grief') to developing epilepsy

Depressive reaction related to family or social stigmatization

Prodromal depression

Depression as an aura

Ictal depression (including partial status)

Post ictal depression

Depression related to control of seizures

people with epilepsy). It is less common than anxiety as a prodrome or as an ictal phenomenon, although post-ictal depression (having all the characteristics of psychotic depression) can be particularly severe, may last longer, and, if the seizures cannot be suppressed, can be very difficult to treat. Suicide attempts have been described in ictal depression.

More people with epilepsy develop depression than would be expected by chance and often seem to do this as seizure frequency is declining or seizures have stopped. There is a possible association between right hemisphere epilepsy and affective illness.

Depression in people with epilepsy is often fairly transient with sudden onset and abrupt departure and may well fluctuate in intensity. These rapid fluctuations with sudden worsening of intensity may, however, be responsible for the increased suicide risk in people (especially young men) with epilepsy and although active treatment can sometimes be avoided or delayed this is only *providing full support and supervision are available*. People with epilepsy who are depressed must be regarded as having an increased suicide risk over people with an equal degree of depression who do not have epilepsy.

If a depression occurring in a patient with epilepsy needs antidepressants or even ECT they should not be withheld. All antidepressants carry some risk of precipitating seizures or increasing their frequency, although this is not a very high risk in patients whose antiepileptic medication is in the therapeutic range (indeed it may be difficult to induce a seizure in such patients with ECT). Choose the anti-depressant that best suits the patient's depression rather than trying to choose the least convulsant one and accept that there may be a temporary slight increase in seizure frequency. Do not be frozen into inactivity in treating a potentially life threatening illness through fear of the epilepsy. Use cognitive therapy and active counselling for the often prolonged grief reactions that occur on the acquisition of either epilepsy or its stigma, and for the depression prone in between episodes.

Hypomania does occur in people with epilepsy,[63] sometimes during flurries of seizures, and may be more common than usually accepted since it is often mistaken for schizophrenia and needs careful distinction from delirium and other organic brain disorders occurring in people with epilepsy. Epilepsy related hypomania usually subsides rapidly with brief treatment with an appropriate neuroleptic such as haloperidol.

Psychoses

Although much less common than depression the psychotic illnesses related to epilepsy have fascinated both neurologists and psychiatrists for nearly one hundred years.[56, 57, 58, 60, 64] Clinicians are keen to disentangle the relationship between the two conditions, in the hope that doing so will illuminate the causation of both: in this hope they may be both deluded and disappointed! Many studies have looked at highly selected populations of patients with epilepsy making the apparent association appear stronger than it probably is: certainly in ordinary psychiatric practice fresh cases of psychosis co-existing with epilepsy are relatively uncommon (only 3% of new admissions of people with epilepsy to psychiatric care, although once admitted such cases tend to remain in care).[55] In a sea of disagreement certain islands of accord are visible:

1. Acute and chronic delusional/hallucinatory psychoses are probably more common in people with epilepsy than would be expected by chance, although the two conditions must occur together by chance sometimes, as they are both common.

2. Most lack the full diagnostic criteria for schizophrenia (particularly because of preservation of affective response), so that they are often called the 'schizophreniform psychoses of epilepsy' rather than schizophrenia.

3. Most — but not all[7] — authorities agree that these states are likely to appear when the epilepsy itself is declining.

4. Most — but not all — authorities agree that these psychoses are unrelated to medication or a genetic propensity to schizophrenia but are related to epileptic foci in the temporal lobe.

5. Some authorities — but certainly not all — consider that epileptic activity in the left temporal lobe is particularly likely to lead to psychosis.

6. Many people with schizophrenia itself have a low convulsive threshold and are particularly likely to develop medication induced seizures.

In practical terms the development of epileptic seizures in a patient with schizophrenia needs full investigation but is likely to be due to medication taken for the schizophrenia (clozaril seems particularly prone to do this). Likewise the development of 'schizophrenia' in a patient with epilepsy warrants full investigation as there is a differential diagnosis:

1. Medication effect/drug intoxication.

2. Metabolic disorder related to anticonvulsants, e.g. folate deficiency/sodium depletion.

3. Recurrent twilight state.

4. Organic brain disease (including progressive dementia, delirium, occult neoplasm).

5. Affective illness (particularly hypomania).

Full investigation would include an EEG recorded during seizures and psychotic episodes (if possible) and a high quality brain MRI.

The treatment of 'schizophrenia' and epilepsy occurring together is often difficult as control of seizures may exacerbate the psychosis and medication used to control the psychosis may exacerbate the epilepsy; often the clinician (with the family and patient) has to decide whether the patient is better off with some psychosis but no epilepsy or with some seizures but sane.

As with depression choose the antipsychotic drug that the patient needs for the psychosis (but try to avoid the more sedating ones). Try to avoid enzyme inducing anticonvulsants and those that are more sedating, also try to avoid those known to make psychosis worse (e.g. vigabatrin, topiramate) and if using clozaril avoid those anti-epileptics that may have a bone marrow/platelet suppressant effect (e.g. carbamazepine, valproate). Lamotrigine and gabapentin are probably the best to use, if possible, in the person with epilepsy who is prone to psychosis.

Organic mental states and epilepsy

Confusion and delirium are common in epilepsy and usually associated with an increase in seizure frequency (usually sudden). In addition to increased psychomotor activity, perceptual distortion (usually visual hallucinations), disorientation and confusion there is often a paranoid element, so that these states are often mistaken for a psychosis.

Dementia is associated with epilepsy partly because some dementing syndromes cause epilepsy (see the section on Aetiology), and partly because many people with severe brain damage (and epilepsy) dement early, but also because there is evidence that some people with severe epilepsy do suffer progressive intellectual loss.[65] The differential diagnosis includes drug intoxication and chronic psychotic illness.

'Twilight states'

Recurrent confusional states (which can last for several weeks) can be caused by *subconvulsive generalized status epilepticus* or by *complex partial status*. These states can be post-ictal but more commonly arise de novo (and may be the first presentation of the underlying epilepsy). *Subconvulsive generalized status* is accompanied by a fluctuating confusion varying from near stupor to mild impairment of cognitive function, sometimes with accompanying irritability or querulousness; psychotic symptoms may be present.

Complex partial status, in which continual epileptic discharge occurs in one temporal lobe, can cause a wide variety of symptoms, usually of a psychotic nature (irritability, psychotic symptoms — including catatonia — wandering and fugue-like states, and neurotic symptoms). A degree of confusion is always present but may not be very obvious. The condition should be suspected in any patient who has a recurrent psychiatric condition with sudden onset and offset with an element of confusion or 'organicity'. The EEG will always be abnormal and intravenous benzodiazepines remove the mental symptoms.

For a full account of the organic mental states of epilepsy see Betts.[7]

Further reading

Mendez M (1996) Disorders of mood and affect in epilepsy. In: *Psychological Disturbances in Epilepsy* (eds J Sackellares and S Berent), Boston: Butterworth-Heinemann, pp. 125–41.

Treiman D (1991) Psychology of ictal aggression: In: *Advances in Neurology No. 55* (eds D Smith, D Treiman and M Trimble), New York: Raven Press, pp. 341–56.

Is it epilepsy? (Non-epileptic seizures) The paroxysmal disorders

16

Sudden paroxysmal changes in behaviour, in thinking and feeling or in contact with or relationship to inner and external reality are a common part of human experience. Sometimes such changes are driven by epileptic mechanisms but often are due to some other physical or psychological phenomenon, but mistaken for epilepsy. The reason for this is that although epilepsy has protean manifestations it has been placed on a kind of diagnostic and therapeutic pedestal, so that when faced with recurrent paroxysmal changes in behaviour, thinking or feeling in a patient, instead of recognizing that there is a wide differential diagnosis we tend to 'think epilepsy', partly because many phenomena of the paroxysmal disorders are, unless analysed properly, vaguely reminiscent of epilepsy, and partly because the diagnosis of epilepsy gives therapeutic promise and respectability to a set of behaviours which would otherwise be threatening and disturbing.

Epilepsy is also overdiagnosed because its initial diagnosis is often made by primary care doctors whose knowledge of the wide differential diagnosis of the paroxysmal disorders is small: once made the diagnosis is difficult to remove. Sander et al showed that in primary care in nearly 30% of patients the diagnosis of epilepsy is difficult and needs time and patience.[14] Precipitate treatment of new onset seizures as epilepsy (often to relieve medical or family anxiety) is wrong.

A non-epileptic seizure has been defined as a 'sudden, usually disruptive, change in a person's behaviour, perception, thinking, or feeling which is usually time limited and which resembles, or is mistaken for, epilepsy but which does not have the characteristic electrophysiological changes detectable by electroencephalography which accompanies a true epileptic seizure'.[66] The term '*pseudoseizure*' is sometimes used to describe the same phenomenon but is both wrong and pejorative and its use is gradually being abandoned.

Prevalence of non-epileptic seizures

Depending on how they were assessed, by whom and where, 5–20% of people with a confident diagnosis of epilepsy turn out later to have some other disorder which has been misdiagnosed. This is particularly likely in tertiary specialist epilepsy practice. Many patients with 'chronic intractable epilepsy' turn out, on fuller assessment, to have largely or exclusively non-epileptic seizures. Misdiagnosis of epilepsy, long perpetuated, is also very likely to occur in the learning disability field, particularly because these patients, most in need of accurate investigation and assessment, are least likely to receive it. In some settings non-epilepsy is extremely common (nearly 50% of patients admitted to casualty in 'status epilepticus' turn out not to have epilepsy).

Since many patients with non-epileptic seizures will be receiving the more expensive treatments for their non-existent epilepsy, the condition is of some economic importance, particularly in the more extreme cases, because of frequent admissions to hospital for treatment.

Classification of non-epileptic seizures

It is not enough to recognize that a patient's seizures are non-epileptic in nature: some attention must be paid to recognize the type of seizure so that the appropriate treatment can be started. There is no universal accepted classification of these disorders and what classifications exist are an untidy mixture of aetiology and description. A summary of the presentation of paroxysmal disorders is presented below. Distinguishing between epileptic and non-epileptic seizures is difficult. Published lists and tables of distinguishing features between epilepsy and non-epilepsy can be misleading. There are no clinical phenomena that are exclusive to epilepsy and no phenomena that occur solely in non-epileptic attacks: everything that happens in epilepsy can also be a feature of non-epileptic attacks and vice versa.[25] The decision as to whether a particular patient's seizures are epileptic or not should only be made after careful and judicious scrutiny of all the evidence.

Even traditionally reliable evidence such as tongue biting, incontinence or injury does not reliably distinguish epileptic from non-epileptic seizures. Tongue biting (usually at the tip) can occur in non-epileptic seizures as can incontinence and injury. Some patients with non-epileptic seizures are inwardly driven to injure and hurt themselves and may be incontinent either better to imitate an epileptic attack or because of some inwardly driven motivation.

> **TONGUE BITING**
>
> *Injuries to the tongue in a seizure may occur at the tip, or at one or both sides, or the cheek may be bitten. Bites at the side of the tongue (some bilateral) are usually seen after a tonic clonic seizure but may occur in complex partial seizures (often, then, unilateral and ipsilateral to the side of the seizure). The cheek may be bitten similarly, both side of tongue and cheek damage can occur in simulation but simulated tongue biting is more usually found at the tip of the tongue. However, the tip of the tongue can also be injured in faints and falls, particularly if the chin is struck. Biting of the lips is also encountered in both complex partial seizures and in non-epileptic seizures.*

Modes of presentation of non-epileptic seizures

Non-epileptic seizures may present as:[7,67]

- Apparent sudden unconsciousness, with no (or very little) movement; possible falling

- Apparent loss of consciousness with convulsive movement, usually but not invariably, bilateral

- Apparent loss or impairment of consciousness with some other motor phenomena

- Apparent loss or impairment of consciousness with emotional or cognitive phenomena

- Attacks without apparent loss of consciousness with some kind of motor, subjective emotional or cognitive experience

- Motor, emotional or cognitive phenomena apparently starting in sleep, usually continuing into waking, with or without apparent impairment of consciousness

Note: In all these presentations the initial, usually brief, event may be an epileptic one and the remainder of the attack a conscious or unconscious elaboration or exaggeration of the original epileptic experience. If medication controls the epilepsy it may not control the rest of the attack.

Apparent sudden unconsciousness with no (or very little) movement: possible falling

This can be caused by epilepsy or by a wide variety of non-epileptic experience, both emotional and organic (**Table 28**). There may be a warning or none. If epilepsy it is usually a primary generalized (tonic or atonic) seizure. In both, recovery of consciousness (unless the patient has injured the head in falling) is swift and there is little postictal confusion (unless, again, the patient's head has been struck in the fall). Sudden loss of consciousness with falling can occur in epilepsy originating in the temporal or frontal lobes. It is usually an atonic fall, although occasionally a tonic spasm can occur (particularly in frontal seizures). Consciousness is usually fairly quickly regained. The patient who falls in a flaccid way and who lies inert, remaining apparently unconscious for some time, is unlikely to have epilepsy. Such falling epileptic seizures, when monitored by an electroencephalogram, may not be detected, either because the patient is in bed and the characteristic fall is not seen or because the fall itself produces such artefact in the recording device that the ictal nature of the event is obscured.

It is also possible that the preliminary collapse was due to epilepsy but the subsequent behaviour is a psychological elaboration of the brief epileptic experience. This is not uncommon because such sudden epileptic drops are frightening for the patient and relatives.

Collapse and unconsciousness can also be a symptom of various organic diseases, mainly

Table 28
Causes of apparent loss of consciousness with little or no movement and possible falling.[7]

Epilepsy

1. Generalized

2. Partial

Other neurological

1. Basilar migraine

2. Meniere's disease

3. Transient ischaemic attack

4. IIIrd ventricle cyst

5. Cataplexy

Cardiovascular

1. Syncope

2. Stokes–Adams attacks and other arrythmias

3. Aortic stenosis

4. Atrial myxoma

5. Mitral valve prolapse?

Other physical

1. Hypoglycaemia

Emotional

1. Emotional syncope

2. Hyperventilation

3. Cutting off (avoidance) behaviour: 'swoon'

4. Catalepsy

neurological and cardiac (**Table 28**). Premonitionary feelings of dizziness or awareness of an oncoming loss of consciousness in these conditions can occasionally be mistaken for prodromes or auras of epilepsy. The commonest physical event that leads to collapse and unconsciousness is *syncope*. This can usu-ally be easily recognized from the history and description of the attack (the patient's characteristic pre-ictal feelings of dizziness, heat and impending collapse beforehand, followed by the characteristic collapse with pallor and sweating). Recovery is usually rapid, but if the person faints (whether from physical or emotional causes) and is kept upright or cannot lie flat then unconsciousness may be prolonged and other neurological symptoms may occur so that the diagnosis becomes difficult. Syncopal attacks can look very neurological,[68] and can occur even when patients are sitting or even lying (particularly in the elderly). Tonic spasms, twitching and incontinence can all occur as part of syncope.

Emotional syncope is induced by the threat of a physical event like blood letting, injection or even by the sight of blood, by talk of unpleasant things or the threat of them. In some people syncope becomes reflex without an obvious precipitant. This can make diagnosis difficult because the patient appears to be spontaneously losing consciousness.

In the same way, although the classical history of rising panic, the characteristic feeling that enough air cannot be got into the lungs, peripheral tingling and tetany plus peri-oral numbness and tingling, will usually suggest *hyperventilation* related loss of consciousness and collapse, patients who *chronically* hyperventilate (common in the anxious) can lose consciousness quickly and fall, apparently unconscious, without the characteristic prodromal feelings. Severe hyperventilation attacks can be accompanied by apparent foaming of the mouth (sialorrhoea, common in severe anxiety). Patients may lie inert and

even cyanosed for some minutes before they start to breath again. This causes great anxiety in onlookers. Tachypnoea (which looks like hyperventilation) can occur in partial seizures and may cause misdiagnosis of epilepsy as non-epilepsy.

'Swooning' is collapse with apparent unconsciousness, with patients closing their eyes, sinking to the floor and lying flaccid and inert, sometimes for long periods of time. Patients do not usually resist passive movement but will usually resist eye opening and eventually recover without many post-ictal symptoms. It is not unlike the 'playing dead' of children and is believed to relate to the mechanism of lying inert and splitting conscious awareness described by Jehu in children being sexually abused.[69] Such victims describe themselves as becoming passive observers of the situation almost as though they are watching events from a corner of the room. This may become a learnt pattern of behaviour in stressful situations or be used as a mechanism for avoiding flashbacks and reawakened memories in patients with a post-traumatic stress disorder related to previous sexual abuse. It may also be seen in somatization and conversion disorder and in dissociative and factitious disorders and malingering. Deliberate simulation of unconsciousness is easy to keep up and, if the patient does not react to external stimuli, difficult to detect.

Apparent loss of consciousness with convulsive movement

Generalized tonic clonic seizures are the commonest cause of this presentation **(Table 29)**. Convulsive movement, sometimes bilateral, sometimes unilateral, sometimes with preservation of consciousness also occurs in sensorimotor and frontal based epilepsy. Frontal attacks are often accompanied by rather bizarre movements and behaviour (such as bicycling movements of the legs, swearing, punching etc.) and it is often difficult to register epileptic activity from scalp EEGs during these seizures: they are often mistaken for non-epileptic attacks.

In people with a low convulsive threshold a tonic clonic seizure may be triggered off by cerebral or physical phenomena which temporarily impair cerebral circulation or interfere with cerebral metabolism. True *syncope*

Table 29
Causes of apparent loss of consciousness with convulsive movement.

A. Epilepsy

1. *Primary generalized (tonic clonic seizures)*
2. *Partial seizures with secondary generalization*
3. *Complex partial seizures (usually frontal)*

B. Symptomatic epilepsy

1. *Exogenous (e.g. drug induced, toxins)*
2. *Endogenous (e.g. hypoglycaemia, anoxia, syncope)*
3. *Emotionally precipitated (e.g. hyperventilation)*

C. Physically based non-epileptic seizures

1. *Syncope*
2. *Hyperventilation*

D. Emotionally based convulsive behaviour

1. *'Abreactive', related to post-traumatic stress disorder*
2. *Imitation, conversion disorder*
3. *Imitation, factitious disorder*
4. *Imitation, deliberate (malingering)*
5. *Imitation or induction (Münchausen's disorder by proxy)*

can trigger off a tonic clonic seizure in the predisposed, syncope can be mistaken for a tonic clonic seizure (particularly when victims of syncope are not laid flat) because it is quite possible to get twitching of the limbs in syncope and also incontinence.

Hypoglycaemic attacks can give rise to tonic clonic seizures although this is probably rare.[70] *Hyperventilation* may trigger off a tonic clonic seizure and it may also be mistaken for it if the tetanic movements of a severe hyperventilation attack are mistaken for tonic clonic movements. The prolonged apnoea and cyanosis after a severe hyperventilation attack and sialorrhoea can be confused with epilepsy.

Apparent loss of consciousness followed by convulsive behaviour (or falling and convulsive behaviour) may be emotionally based. The phenomenon of the '*tantrum*' should be well recognized: rather like swooning it resembles childhood behaviour. The victim falls, kicks, screams and struggles and may appear out of contact with his or her surroundings. In the learning disabled such behaviour may be a non-verbal expression of rage or frustration. However caused, such behaviour if reinforced and rewarded can persist for long periods of time particularly in the socially disadvantaged or the learning dis-

abled. It superficially resembles epilepsy, it often seems easier to treat it with medication as though it were, than to unravel the emotions and feelings that lie behind this behaviour.

Swoons may occur in response to unpleasant intrusion of memories or flashbacks of traumatic events, similar mechanisms can lead to a convulsive struggle, the so called *abreactive attack*. This too seems to be particularly associated with women who have been sexually abused as children.[71] The abreactive attack is one of the classic stereotypes of the 'pseudoseizure' with back arching, pelvic thrusting and gasping plus incoordinate body movements (which bear a passing resemblance to sexual activity). Frontal epileptic seizures can look similar but the abreactive attack is usually prolonged whereas frontal lobe seizures are brief and stereotyped. It may well represent the acting out of a flashback in a patient with a chronic post-traumatic stress disorder.[72]

Convulsive behaviour may be imitated, apparently unconsciously, in *conversion disorder* or consciously in *factitious* disorder or *malingering*. Imitated epilepsy is usually based on the laymen's image of epilepsy and it tends to be a wild uncoordinated convulsive struggle with much noise. However, patients may imitate the remembered attacks of friends. People who deliberately imitate epilepsy, either to maintain the sick role or for gain, will often present a much more polished and studied performance.

Non-convulsive attacks, with or without apparent loss of consciousness with motor, emotional or cognitive symptoms (Tables 30 and 31)

The non-epileptic forms of convulsion, whether organically or psychologically based, are often preceded by prodromal symptoms and signs which may be mistaken for the prodromes and auras of epilepsy. Syncope, for instance, can be preceded by a hot dizzy feeling which the patient may not recognize as characteristic of fainting: a rising feeling of anxiety occurs before hyperventilation attacks. During a hyperventilation attack, before loss of consciousness, tingling of the limbs and around the mouth may give the impression of an aura as may changes in emotional feeling before tantrums or abreactive attacks. Peri-oral numbness or tingling is uncommon as an aura of epilepsy but common during or before hyperventilation attacks (and also migraine).

Other emotional, cognitive and behavioural changes that take place in a paroxysmal way, sometimes with apparent alterations in consciousness, may be mistaken for epilepsy. Epilepsy obviously, usually partial, but sometimes primary generalized, can give rise to a rich variety of experiences in which there are sudden changes in awareness, consciousness, cognition, emotion or behaviour, some of which may be quite frightening or puzzling (as in sensorimotor or frontal seizures). Such activity is usually brief but *sub-convulsive generalized status* or *simple partial* or *complex partial status* may continue the behaviour for longer periods of time and can thus imitate some of the symptoms of mental illness quite closely.

Sudden changes in cognitive function can occur as a result of cerebrovascular changes such as a *cortical stroke* or a *transient ischaemic attack*, or occasionally in *migraine*. Recurrent attacks of *hypoglycaemia* may produce acute cognitive, behavioural or emotional changes. Sudden paroxysmal changes induced by *phaeochromocytomas* or the *carcinoid syndrome* may also be occasionally mistaken for cerebral events of an epileptic kind. Unusual or complex *tics*, some of the manifestations of *Tourette's syndrome*, may also be mistaken for epilepsy as can recurrent *paroxysmal dystonias* and other movement disorders.[70]

Table 30
Causes of apparent loss or impairment of consciousness with some other motor phenomena or emotional or cognitive phenomena.

A. Epilepsy
1. Primary generalized
2. Complex partial seizures
3. Sub-convulsive (generalized) status
4. Complex partial status (twilight state)

B. Neurological
1. Transient ischaemic attack
2. Cortical stroke
3. Cataplexy
4. Hypoglycaemia

C. Emotional
1. Fugue (depressive)
2. Fugue (conversion)
3. Episodic dyscontrol syndrome
4. Cataplexy

Table 31
Causes of attacks without apparent loss of consciousness with some kind of motor, emotional or cognitive experience.

A. Epilepsy
1. Primary generalized epilepsy
2. Simple partial seizures
3. Simple partial status

B. Neurological
1. Cortical stroke
2. Transient ischaemic attacks
3. Movement disorders
4. Unusual tics: Tourette's syndrome
5. Hypoglycaemia
6. Phaeochromocytoma/carcinoid
7. Migraine phenomena

C. Emotional
1. Fugue (depressive)
2. Fugue (conversion)
3. Anxiety/depressive phenomena
4. Psychotic phenomena
5. Episodic dyscontrol syndrome

Paroxysmal changes in feeling or internal awareness resembling those of epilepsy are commonly found in people who are stressed, highly aroused, anxious or depressed.[73] Symptoms typical of an aura originating in the temporal lobe (déjà vu, derealization, depersonalization, sudden changes in the perception of taste or smell) are also commonly found in the anxious, the depressed and in people who may have a psychotic illness. In severe *depression* and in *psychotic illness* olfactory or gustatory hallucinations or experiences are common and can be thought to be epileptic. People who hyperventilate often develop a metallic taste in their mouth or a perversion of their sense of smell: this is not epilepsy. The olfactory or gustatory experiences that occur in people who are anxious or depressed lack the intensity and brevity of the epileptic experience: in the epileptic attack something else recognizably epileptic is usually going on at the same time.

People with recurrent, intense auditory or visionary hallucinations occurring as part of a psychotic illness, or who have the peculiar vivid visual hallucinations of cerebrovascular disease *peduncular hallucinosis* or with vivid pseudo hallucinatory experiences may occasionally be thought to have epilepsy, as may people who wander off in a *fugue*. Fugues are rarely epileptic but usually occur as part of a conversion or dissociative phenomenon or in a depressive or psychotic illness. Epileptic fugues occur during an ordinary journey for which the patient has no recollection. The fugue occurs *during* the journey rather than the journey occurring as a consequence of the fugue.[70]

Patients who are repeatedly paroxysmally *aggressive* may sometimes be given a mistaken diagnosis of epilepsy. Ictal rage is rare: when it does occur it is brief, it is undirected, the patient has complete amnesia for it, it is stereotyped and is almost invariably unprovoked.[74] Patients in the middle of a complex partial seizure, if inappropriately challenged or handled, may react aggressively, but there is good evidence that aggression is no more common in epilepsy than it is in the general population. People with apparent aggressive episodes related either to brain damage or to personality disorders may have minor EEG abnormalities but this does not mean that they have epilepsy.

Motor, emotional or cognitive phenomena apparently starting in sleep

Epileptic seizures are common in sleep; it is being increasingly recognized that some of the bizarre behaviours occurring during sleep, formerly thought to be a primary sleep or movement disorder or psychogenic, probably have an epileptic basis to them. However behaviour resembling epileptic seizures can also occur as part of a primary sleep disorder or as a manifestation of psychogenic, cognitive or dissociative events occurring during sleep itself. It is widely believed by clinicians that an attack which starts in sleep cannot be a non-epileptic attack but this is just not true (**Table 32**).

Table 32
Causes of motor, perceptual emotional or cognitive phenomena apparently starting in sleep.

A. At sleep onset
1. Hypnogogic hallucinations
2. Anxiety attacks
3. Sudden bodily jerks (motor sleep start)
4. Myoclonic jerks

B. In early sleep (first 1–2 hours)
1. Night terrors
2. Sleep walking
3. Partial (with or without secondary generalization) seizures
4. Sleep apnoea
5. Restless legs syndrome
6. Periodic movements of sleep
7. Rythmic movement disorder of sleep
8. Sandifer's syndrome (reflux)

C. Mid-late sleep (2–8 hours)
1. Partial (with or without secondary generalization) seizures
2. REM sleep disorder
3. Sleep paralysis
4. Sleep apnoea
5. Dream anxiety disorder (nightmares)
6. Restless legs syndrome
7. Periodic movements of sleep: rhythmic movements of sleep
8. Sandifer's syndrome (reflux)

D. Waking
1. Tonic clonic seizures
2. Myoclonic jerks
3. Hypnopompic hallucinations

Note: these time relationships may not be seen in patients who are seriously sleep deprived, or with disrupted sleep rhythms. Dissociation and conversion phenomena can occur in any sleep stage (usually when the patient is actually awake but appears asleep)

Primary generalized tonic clonic seizures are not uncommon in sleep, usually in the early hours of the morning shortly before or during waking. Most tonic clonic seizures that occur at other times in the sleep cycle are more likely to be secondarily generalized from a partial focus. Other manifestations of primary generalized epilepsy are not usually seen in sleep; it is generally held that myoclonic jerks of an epileptic nature will subside and rarely be apparent in sleep itself, although may be present either when the person is falling asleep or at the point of wakening. Complex partial and simple partial seizures are common in sleep (10–20% of people with epilepsy only have seizures whilst asleep).

It is of course possible for people to have numerous partial seizures in their sleep (and even tonic clonic seizures) and be entirely unaware of them — this is also true for their sleeping partner who may only be woken when a tonic clonic seizure supervenes. Autonomic events seem particularly common in sleep related partial seizures (such as cessation of breathing, intense sweating, cardiac arrhythmias, etc.). Seizure discharge originating in the frontal lobes may produce extremely bizarre bilateral motor behaviour such as spitting, swearing and complex motor behaviours such as getting out of bed, wandering or dancing. Patients with sleep related partial seizures may remember part of their

seizure (particularly if it starts as a simple partial seizure) as a dream experience.

Thus, because of the difficulty of witness observation, the sometimes bizarre experiences that occur during sleep related epileptic seizures and the resemblance of some forms of sleep related epilepsy to other sleep disorders the diagnosis of epilepsy occurring in sleep can be difficult (particularly because the focus of the epileptic activity may be in the frontal lobes: EEG registration of epileptic activity during frontal seizures with scalp electrodes may not occur, even though the seizure is an epileptic one). Sleep related epileptic seizures also share with many of the parasomnias a tendency to occur in clusters with long intervals of seizure free activity in between; they can also, as can the parasomnias, be stress related or environmentally precipitated.

If it is sometimes difficult to recognize that bizarre behviour occurring in the night is actually epilepsy related, it can be equally difficult to distinguish a parasomnia from an epileptic experience. The parasomnias, usually associated with abnormalities of arousal occurring during sleep, are often mistakenly diagnosed as epilepsy. *Sleep walking* and *night terrors* occurring in children are usually recognized for what they are although night terrors, being comparatively brief, paroxysmal and stereotyped and the child often appearing awake but out of touch, may be mistaken for epilepsy. Night terrors occurring in the setting of a normal sleep cycle tend to occur one or two hours after the person has fallen asleep (during the first episode of stage four sleep) but this diagnostically useful time relationship is not seen in people who have marked sleep disturbance.

Sleep walking also occurs in adults, particularly men: usually there will be a history of sleep walking as a child. If it arises de novo there is usually precipitating stress or evidence of disturbed psychopathology. Sleep walkers, although they have their eyes open, appear to be unconscious; they may carry out elaborate and bizarre behaviours and have amnesia for the episode the following morning . The condition can easily be mistaken for epilepsy: sometimes only an ambulatory EEG recording can tell the difference. (Ambulatory EEG recording is helpful not only to register epileptic activity but also to show the sleep stage in which the phenomenon occurs.)

Adult night terrors, which again tend to occur in early stage four sleep, are also episodic and paroxysmal: the apparently terrified victim cannot be roused and may have no recollection of the attack the following morning. *Acute panic disorder* can occur in sleep in adults, usually shortly after the person has

fallen asleep: it wakens the victim who has a clear recollection of it. Both can be confused with epilepsy.

Sleep apnoea can also be mistaken for epilepsy — the sudden start, jerk and snort that occur in sleep apnoea can have a superficial resemblance to partial epilepsy. Similar behaviour related to gastro-oesophageal reflux (often accompanied by bizarre posturing, *Sandifer's syndrome*)[75] can also be mistaken for epilepsy particularly in the learning impaired. Patients having frequent partial seizures in the night, even if they are totally unaware of them, may have daytime drowsiness and sleepiness and thus be thought to have episodes of sleep apnoea.

Rapid eye movement sleep disorder (in which the normal paralysis of dream sleep is absent so that the victim acts out his or her dreams often with violent and destructive behaviour) has also been mistaken for frontal epilepsy. This disorder tends to occur in the later stages of sleep when rapid eye movement sleep is more prominent. It can be difficult to distinguish it both from sleep walking (in which violent behaviour may also occur) and from frontal lobe epileptic discharge.

Since apparent dreaming may be a feature of partial seizures occurring in sleep it is not surprising that sometimes repetitive vivid dreams occurring as part of a *dream anxiety disorder* may be mistaken for epilepsy particularly if the dream is the same on each occasion. Patients with *sleep paralysis* who awaken out of dream sleep unable to move, with a vivid hallucinatory experience and intense fear, may also be mistakenly thought to have epilepsy. This may also happen in patients with *hypnogogic* or *hypnopompic hallucinations*, particularly if they are frequent and of a stereotyped nature. Narcoleptic and cataleptic attacks during waking (which may, at night, be accompanied by hypnogogic or hypnopompic hallucinations and sleep paralysis) have been mistaken for epilepsy.

Movement disorders occurring in sleep may be mistaken for epilepsy. Everyone has experienced sudden bodily jerks on falling asleep (*motor sleep start*) which is normal and physiological, but *periodic movements of sleep (nocturnal myoclonus* — a condition in which there are frequent periodic contractions of leg muscles sometimes associated with arousal) can be mistaken for epilepsy, particularly the more severe forms in which movement of other parts of the body may occur. A similar condition is *rhythmic movement disorder of sleep* in which, during sleep, stereotyped movements of the head or limbs and body rocking may occur. This is common in childhood and may persist into adult life and may

be mistaken for epilepsy. The *restless legs syndrome* has also been mistaken for epilepsy.

A group of movement disorders occurring in sleep (*hypnogenic paroxysmal dystonia, familial paroxysmal hypnogenic dystonia*) were originally thought to be movement disorders unrelated to epilepsy but are now recognized as probable frontal lobe seizures. *Recurrent paroxysmal behaviour disturbance in sleep* (disturbing either to the victim or his or her sleeping partner) is common, may be epileptic in nature, may be part of a primary sleep disorder or a psychological disorder (*dream anxiety disorder*, the nightmares and arousals of *post-traumatic stress disorder, dissociative states*, etc.). These are often difficult to distinguish from each other and often need neurophysiological investigation for correct diagnosis and management.[76]

Psychiatric disorders associated with non-epileptic seizures

Anxiety disorders

Panic attacks and hyperventilation may be mistaken for epilepsy. In those people with chronic anxiety and hyperventilation the induction period before the event is short and may pass unrecognized or is mistaken for a prodrome or an aura. People in a state of chronic hyperventilation often only need to overbreathe for a very short period of time before they develop tetany and collapse.

Patients with generalized anxiety disorders may also be mistakenly diagnosed as having epilepsy if the symptoms of their anxiety resemble temporal lobe phenomena.[73] Sudden intrusive memories (flashbacks) can be mistaken for epilepsy because of their suddenness and intensity and because often during the flashback the patient may act out his or her distress; the intensity of the experience detaches them from their surroundings so that they may appear to be in a complex partial seizure. Epilepsy can sometimes cause a post-traumatic stress disorder (if a seizure leads to a life threatening event) and an unpleasant event (e.g. sexual abuse) can precipitate a patient's first seizure.[77]

Mood disorder

Depression is found more commonly than expected by chance in people with non-epileptic seizures.[78] Depression releases behaviours previously suppressed akin to those in conversion disorder.[79]

Somatization disorder

Ten per cent of a sample of patients with this disorder had non-epileptic seizures,[80] usually of a convulsive type. In Ford's study 50% of

the entire sample had '*blackouts*' that might also have been given a diagnosis of epilepsy.

Conversion disorder

This is a syndrome traditionally associated with non-epileptic seizures[81] and it is likely that previous sexual abuse is a frequent cause.[71] As in somatization disorder about 10% of patients with established conversion disorder have non-epileptic seizures but many more patients probably have 'blackouts'. Non-epileptic seizures are commoner in patients with chronic conversion disorder rather than acute.

Dissociation

This is defined as a disruption in the integrated function of consciousness memory and perception. It, too, can present with symptoms resembling epilepsy (e.g. fugue, depersonalization and amnesia). Such states may sometimes be mistaken for epilepsy; it is likely that 'swoons' are commoner in people who have disclosed a previous history of sexual abuse as a child.[71]

Factitious disorder

This is the deliberate simulation of physical or psychological illness in order to remain in the sick role. Some patients simulate epilepsy as part of this disorder although the frequency of this behaviour in factitious disorder is uncertain. It is likely that pseudo status epilepticus is particularly commonly associated with this disorder.[82] Factitious disorder, although deliberate, is inwardly driven and may be out of the patient's control. *Factitious disorder by proxy*, the intentional induction or false reporting of physical or psychological illness in a dependent person is rarely a cause of apparent epilepsy in children and may be induced by misuse of medication or insulin, but more usually by semi smothering.[83]

Malingering

This is the deliberate production of signs and symptoms of illness for gain. Some patients with non-epileptic seizures belong to this category, although not as commonly as is usually supposed.

Recognition of non-epileptic seizures

In assessing patients with newly presenting seizures and those whose intractable epilepsy is being reviewed keep a high index of suspicion and always ask yourself 'is this really epilepsy?'. Epileptic attacks tend to be stereotyped and brief, non-epileptic attacks may be prolonged, relatively non-stereotyped and behaviour in them may be modified by the actions of the observer. But very bizarre behaviour may occur in some temporal, sensorimotor and, particularly, frontal seizures and behaviour can look very '*psychiatric*'. There is no feature of a seizure that invariably distinguishes between epilepsy and non-epilepsy, although as we develop a descriptive phenomenology based on analysis of video-taped seizure activity reliable clues to the provenance of seizures may develop. Some features of an attack are more in keeping with a non-epileptic seizure, related to characteristic muscle movements — head and neck thrashing without bodily movements for instance.[84] One other physical sign that is sometimes helpful is the patient who is out of breath at the end of a seizure.[81] It should be remembered that tongue biting, injury and incontinence (even fecal incontinence) do not always distinguish epilepsy from non-epilepsy.

Diagnosis of non-epileptic seizures

Diagnosis should never be hurried and should never be a '*knee jerk*' reaction to one particular feature of the seizure. The diagnosis depends upon judicious consideration of a full medical, neurological and psychiatric history and examination. There should be a careful appraisal of the seizure history complemented, where possible, by ancillary investigation of seizure phenomenology. The diagnosis of non-epileptic attacks remains a *clinical* diagnosis and should not be driven purely by the results of physical investigations which may be misleading. **It is possible to be 100% sure that a seizure is an epileptic one; it is rarely possible to be completely certain that it is not.**

Diagnosis is based on a hierarchy of investigations:

> **Seizure history**
>
> **Seizure observation**
>
> **Seizure registration/video**
>
> **Post-ictal prolactin levels**
>
> **Post-ictal EEG**
>
> **Ambulatory monitoring of ictal EEG (plus video, if possible)**
>
> **Telemetered monitoring of ictal EEG, with video if possible**
>
> **Ictal EEG using telemetry and invasive electrodes (e.g. subdural strips)**

Seizure history and description may not be accurate; the account of both the victim and the witness may be seriously flawed. Witnesses may be too frightened to observe properly and the description of what was seen distorted by anxiety. *Observation* of the seizure by a trained person is better but may also be misleading. *Seizure registration on video tape* is perhaps the most helpful form of observation, particularly as the seizure can then be analysed at leisure. The availability of inexpensive video recorders means that families or friends can (with some instruction) make recordings at home where seizures are much more likely to occur — this is particularly helpful in the learning disability field.

Prolactin[23]

Blood levels taken 20 minutes after the *onset* of a seizure can be helpful: after generalized convulsive seizures prolactin levels rise many times above baseline levels, after complex partial seizures there is often a two to three fold rise above baseline. Unfortunately this test is not helpful in frontal seizures. A comparison baseline prolactin level taken at the same time of day when seizure activity is not present is essential and it is important to remember that the prolactin rise may not be seen if a second seizure follows quickly on the first.[23]

Post-ictal EEG recording

If a suspected seizure occurs in hospital and EEG facilities are immediately available then a post-ictal recording after a convulsive seizure may be helpful, and characteristic post-ictal changes occur (their absence is not diagnostic) **(Figure 11b)**.

Ictal EEG recording

This is helpful with concomitant video recording if possible, if the patient is having a sufficient number of seizures to make such a recording economical. Ambulatory EEG recording has the advantage of being able to record the patient in his or her natural setting where seizures are more likely to occur. However, artefact and the limited number of electrodes reduce the efficacy of this investigatory tool. Telemetered EEG recording in hospital is more accurate but is extremely costly. It is possible, in hospital, to withdraw medication (but it is important to make sure that any seizures induced by drug withdrawal are the same as the patient's usual seizures). In some complex partial and simple partial seizures, particularly frontal seizures, epileptic activity may not be recorded from scalp electrodes.

Invasive EEG electrodes are more accurate in detecting epileptic activity in some complex partial and simple partial seizures but have a morbidity and a potential mortality and are not usually used to differentiate between epileptic and non-epileptic seizures (although they have been shown to do this).[25]

Suggestion

It is possible, by using injections of normal saline or alcohol soaked patches placed on the neck, to induce non-epileptic seizures in patients by suggestion; most authorities feel that this can reliably distinguish between epilepsy and non-epilepsy.[85] It would be important to make sure that such induced seizures were similar to the patient's usual ones. This is a technique widely used in the USA but little in the UK because of perceived ethical difficulties and distortion to the doctor/patient relationship.

Psychological tests

Some clinicians rely on the MMPI (the Minnesota multiphasic personality inventory) to distinguish between patients with non-epileptic seizures and patients with genuine epileptic seizures,[86] although the use of this technique has been criticized and it is little used in the UK.

General management of non-epileptic seizures

Once a diagnosis of non-epileptic seizures has been made on clinical grounds as certainly as possible, the patient should be prepared for the change in diagnosis and not suddenly rejected or referred to the nearest psychiatrist (who will only refer them straight back).

What to say to the patient

Direct confrontation with 'the truth' is usually unhelpful. It is generally better to leave the patients to recognize for themselves that some or all of their attacks are not epilepsy (many already know or suspect and may be relieved to be told gently). The doctor should say something like 'I am glad that we now know that these are emotional attacks, because it means you can be helped to overcome them'.

Precipitating factors

These need to be looked for and enquired about. The circumstances of the first 'fit' may be helpful. Primary or secondary gain may be obvious or the attack's symbolic meaning may become apparent once a patient becomes well known to you. In some cases abreaction may be helpful (e.g. showing the patient their attack on video). In female patients in particular, enquiries about sexual trauma, specifically incest, may be needed but should not become a witchhunt.[77] Behavioural analysis is helpful for investigating unintentional or intentional reinforce-

ment of the attack behaviour and family response to the attacks should be assessed critically.

Staff, fellow patients and family should ignore the attacks and avoid rewarding them. This usually results in the frequency of attacks rising to a peak, and then falling precipitously. Praise — positive reinforcement — should be given to attack free periods. Medication should be slowly withdrawn or, if the non-epileptic attacks are combined with epilepsy, rationalized to monotherapy. If the patient is not allowed to keep his or her dignity and self respect, attacks will continue.

Specific management

Anxiety and panic attacks need intensive behavioural treatment (occasionally antidepressants are helpful). The episodic dyscontrol syndrome (outbursts of rage and aggression with minimal precipitation, often appearing in patients with a non-specific EEG abnormality) is best helped by counselling, anger management, environmental manipulation and occasionally by treatment with major tranquillizers or carbamazepine.

Patients with non-epileptic attacks related to sexual abuse are best helped by behavioural management coupled with explanatory psychotherapy and abuse counselling. Seizure frequency may well rise during critical moments in the counselling and must be expected.

Tantrums should be handled by negative reinforcement coupled with reinforcement of attack free behaviour (operant conditioning). Non-epileptic seizures occurring in conversion disorders and somataform disorders are best treated by trying to avoid reinforcement and secondary gain, reinforcing the absence of attacks and using counselling or psychotherapy to explore the underlying reasons for the behaviour. Most patients with factitious disorder when discovered leave medical care abruptly but some, with patient handling, can gain insight into their condition.

It should be remembered that in many ways all the principles of management outlined above can apply equally to the psychological management of genuine epilepsy and since it is possible to get the diagnosis of non-epilepsy wrong this may be a very comforting reflection.

Pitfalls in diagnosing epilepsy in the learning impaired

Epilepsy may be difficult to recognize in people with learning difficulty so that a false diagnosis of non-epilepsy is made. Much more commonly behaviour which is not epileptic but may be paroxysmal in nature is often labelled as epilepsy. The prevalence of non-epileptic seizures in the learning disabled population (although never measured) is probably higher than that in the non-learning-impaired population. The reason for this is twofold: first, emotionally and psychologically driven behaviour often appears in the learning disabled in a paroxysmal manner, but the emotional or environmental cues that drive it are not noticed. Paroxysmal disturbed behaviour if labelled as epileptic or organic can then be given medical treatment. Second, people with learning difficulty are subject to other organic and behavioural phenomena which are commonly mislabelled as epilepsy **(see Table 33)**.

Epilepsy is sometimes not recognized in the learning disabled because seizures may go on longer than normal, in patients whose brains lack the usual compensatory and inhibitory mechanisms. Multiple seizures are common with resultant exhaustion of the prolactin response; reflex epilepsies do occur in the learning disabled population but are often unnoticed because a patient lacks the verbal skills to describe what precipitates the seizure.

Severe brain disorganization may lead to bizarre or atypical presentations of an epileptic seizure so that it is not recognized. Since many patients with learning difficulties lack

Table 33
Phenomena mistaken for epilepsy
in the learning impaired. All these
modalities of sudden paroxysmal
change in behaviour have, in the
author's experience, been mistaken for epilepsy in the learning
impaired.

Severe persistent EEG abnormality (mislabelled 'status')
Dystonias, head movements/nodding
Tongue thrusting
Abnormal postural reflexes (opisthotonos) or tonic neck reflex
Stereotypical behaviours:
chewing
buccal
autistic
Eye movement/deviation/nystagmus
Respiratory phenomena:
tachypnoea
apnoea
periodic breathing
Startle phenomena
Myoclonic phenomena (non-epileptic)
Sleep phenomena

verbal skills they may be unable to describe prodromal symptoms or auras, but respond behaviourally to them; this behavioural response is then misidentified as non-epileptic behaviour. The need for a carer to get to know the patient well is very important.

Another reason for the non-recognition of epilepsy in the learning disabled is the fact that they are often not exposed to modern investigatory techniques (see the section on investigation).

Further reading

Betts T (1994) Management of psychogenic and pseudo epileptic seizures. In: *Epileptic Seizures and Syndromes* (ed P Wolf), Chichester: John Wiley & Sons, pp. 649–56.

Kalogjera-Sackellares D (1996) Psychological disturbances in patients with pseudoseizures. In: *Psychological Disturbances in Epilepsy* (eds J Sackellares and S Berent), Boston: Butterworth-Heinemann, pp. 191–218.

References

1. During M and Spencer D (1993) Extracellular hippocampal glutamate and spontaneous seizures in the human brain. *Lancet* **341**: 1607–1610.

2. Lockard JS (1980) A primate model of clinical epilepsy: mechanisms of action through quantification of therapeutic effects. In: *Epilepsy: A Window to Brain Mechanisms* (ed. JS Lockard and AA Ward), pp. 11–49. New York: Raven Press.

3. Schwartzkroin P, Moshe S, Noebels J and Swann J (ed.) (1995). *Brain Development and Epilepsy*. New York: Oxford University Press.

4. Morgan J and Curran T (1991) Stimulus transcription coupling in the nervous system: involvement of the inducible proto-oncogenes *fos* and *jun*. *Ann Rev Neurosci* **14**: 421–451.

5. Larkin M (1997) Epilepsy genes signal new targets for therapy. *Lancet* **349**: 626.

6. Appleton R and Gibbs J (1995) *Epilepsy in Childhood and Adolescence.* London: Martin Dunitz.

7. Betts T (1993) Neuropsychiatry. In: *A Textbook of Epilepsy* (ed. J Laidlaw, A Richens and D Chadwick). Edinburgh: Churchill Livingstone.

8. Anderson W and Hauser W (1993) Genetics. In: *A Textbook of Epilepsy* (ed. J Laidlaw, A Richens and D Chadwick), pp. 47–75. Edinburgh: Churchill Livingstone.

9. The Tuberous Sclerosis Association (1994) *Tuberous Sclerosis ... more than just skin deep.* Booklet obtainable from the Tuberous Sclerosis Association, Little Barnsley Farm, Catshill, Bromsgrove, Worcestershire, UK B61 ONQ.

10. Gomez M (ed.) (1979) *Tuberous Sclerosis.* New York: Raven Press.

11. Walsh C (1995) Neuronal identity, neuronal migration and epileptic disorders of the cerebral cortex. In: *Brain Development and Epilepsy* (ed. P Schwartzkroin, S Moshe, J Noebell and J Swann). New York: Oxford University Press.

12. Meencke HJ (1994) Minimal developmental disturbances in epilepsy and MRI. In: *Magnetic Resonance Scanning and Epilepsy* (ed. S Shorvon, D Fish, G Bydder et al. New York: Plenum Press.

13. Parker A, Agathonikou A and Panayiotopoulos C (1997) An aggressive seizure and behavioural disorder following trivial head injury. *Seizure* **6**: in press.

14. Sander JW, Hart YM, Johnson AC and Shorvon SD (1990) National general practice study of epilepsy: newly diagnosed epileptic seizures in a general population. *Lancet* **336**: 1267–1271.

15. Cohen BH (1993) Metabolic and degenerative diseases associated with epilepsy. *Epilepsia* **34** (Suppl. 3): 562–570.

16. Hopkins A, Shorvon S (1995) Definitions and epidemiology of epilepsy. In: *Epilepsy* (ed. A Hopkins, S Shorvon and F Cascino), 2nd edn, pp. 1–24. London: Chapman & Hall.

17. Goodridge D and Shorvon S (1983) Epileptic seizures in a population of 6,000. 1) Demography, diagnosis and classification and role of the hospital services. *Br Med J* **287**: 641–644.

18. Hauser W, Annegers J and Karland L (1993) Incidence of epilepsy in unprovoked seizures in Rochester, Minnesota, 1935–1984. *Epilepsia* **34**: 453–68.

19. Sadzot B (1997) Epilepsy: a progressive disease? *Br Med J* **314**: 391.

20. Nashef L and Sander J (1996) Sudden unexpected deaths in epilepsy — where are we now? *Seizure* **5**: 235–238.

21. Commission on classification and terminology of the International League Against Epilepsy 1981. A proposal for a revised seizure classification. *Epilepsia* **22**: 489–501.

22. Commission on classification and terminology of the International League Against Epilepsy 1989. A proposal for the classification of epilepsy and epileptic syndromes. *Epilepsia* **30**: 389–399.

23. Pritchard P (1993) The role of prolactin in the diagnosis of non-epileptic seizures. In: *Non-epileptic Seizures* (ed. A Rowan and J Gates). Boston: Butterworth-Heinemann.

24. Brown S, Betts T, Chadwick D et al (1993) An epilepsy needs document. *Seizure* **2**: 91–103.

25. Wyler A, Hermann B, Blumer D et al (1993) Pseudo- pseudo epileptic seizures. In: *Non-epileptic Seizures* (ed. A Rowan, and J Gates), pp. 73–84. Boston: Butterworth-Heinmann.

26. Turnbull L (1994) Magnetic resonance angiography: principles and clinical application. *Br J Hosp Med* **51** (4): 154–160.

27. Kuzniecky R and Jackson G (1995) *Magnetic Resonance Imaging in Epilepsy.* New York: Raven Press.

28. Jacoby A, Baker G, Steen N et al (1996) The clinical course of epilepsy and its psychosocial correlates. *Epilepsia* **37**: 148–161.

29. Brodie M, Richens A and Yuen A (1995) Double blind comparison of lamotrigine and carbamazepine in newly diagnosed epilepsy. *Lancet* **345**: 476–479.

30. Chadwick D et al (1997) Gabapentin monotherapy in patients with newly diagnosed epilepsy: results of a double-blind fixed dose study comparing three doses of gabapentin and open label carbamczcpinc. Presented at the 22nd International Epilepsy Congress, Dublin.

31. Betts T and Smith K (1996) Epilepsy, primary care and the new therapies. *Rev Contemp Pharmacother* **7**: 239–248.

32. Tallis R (1995) *Epilepsy in Elderly People*, London: Martin Dunitz.

33. MRC Antiepileptic Drug Withdrawal Study Group 1993. Prognostic index for recurrence of seizures after remission of epilepsy. *Br Med J* **306**: 1374–1378.

34. Wolfe P (1995) Non-medical treatment of first epileptic seizures in adolescence and adulthood. *Seizure* **4**: 87–94.

35. Betts T (1992) Epilepsy and stress. *Br Med J* **305**: 378–379.

36. Fenwick P (1991) Evocation and inhibition of seizures — behavioural treatment. In: *Advances in Neurology No 55: Neurobehavioural Problems in Epilepsy* (ed. D Smith, D Treiman and M Trimble), pp.163–183. New York: Raven Press.

37. Harding G and Jeavons P (1994) *Photosensitive Epilepsy — New Edition Clinics in Developmental Medicine No. 133*. London: Mackleth Press.

38. Forster F (1972) The classification and conditioning treatment of the reflex epilepsies. *Int J Neurol* **9**: 73–86.

39. Dahl J, Melin J and Lund L (1987) Effects of a contingent relaxation treatment program on adults with refactory epileptic seizures. *Epilepsia* **28**: 125–132.

40 Mostofsky D and Balaschak B (1997) Psychobiological control of seizures. *Psychol Bull* **84**: 723–759.

41. Dahl J (1992) *Epilepsy: a Behaviour Medicine Approach to Assessment and Treatment in Children*. Seattle: Hogrefe and Huber.

42. Brown S (1995) Other treatments for epilepsy. In: *Epilepsy* (ed. A Hopkins, S Shorvon and G Cascino), 2nd edn. London: Chapman & Hall Medical.

43. Betts T and MacCullum R (1998) Experience of a 'smell memory' technique for the self control of epilepsy. *Seizure* **7**: in press.

44. Cummings L, Giudice L and Morrell M (1995) Ovulatory function in epilepsy. *Epilepsia* **36**: 353.

45. Herzog A (1996) Polycystic ovary syndrome in women with epilepsy: epileptic or iatrogenic? *Ann Neurol* **39**: 559.

46. Webber M, Hauser H, Ottman R and Annegers J (1986) Fertility in persons with epilepsy 1935–1974. *Epilepsia* **27**: 746.

47. Schupf N and Ottman R (1994) The likelihood of pregnancy in individuals with idiopathic/cryptogenic epilepsy: social and biological influences. *Epilepsia* **35**: 750.

48. Krauss G, Brandt J, Campbell M *et al* (1996) Antiepileptic medication and oral contraceptive interactions: A national survey of neurologists and obstetricians. *Neurology* 46: 1534.

49. Morrell M and Guldner G (1996) Self-reported sexual function and sexual arousability in women with epilepsy. *Epilepsia* **37**: 1204.

50. Dansky L (1995) The teratogenic effects of epilepsy and anticonvulsant drugs in epilepsy. In: *Epilepsy* (ed. A Hopkins, S Shorvon and G Cascino), 2nd edn, pp. 535–555. London: Chapman & Hall Medical.

51. Hopkins A (1995) Epilepsy, menstruation, oral contraception and pregnancy. In: *Epilepsy* (ed. A Hopkins, S Shorvon and G Cascino), 2nd edn, pp. 521–533. London: Chapman & Hall Medical.

52. Morrell M (1996) The new antiepileptic drugs and women: Efficacy, reproductive health, pregnancy and fetal outcome. *Epilepsia* **37** (Suppl 6): S34.

53. Kirkham F (1995) Epilepsy and mental retardation. In: *Epilepsy* (ed. A Hopkins, S Shorvon and G Cascino), 2nd edn, pp. 503–520. London: Chapman & Hall Medical.

54. Giordani B (1996) Intellectual and cognitive disturbances in epileptic patients. In: *Psychological Disturbances in Epilepsy* (ed. J Sackellares and S Brent), pp. 45–97. Boston: Butterworth-Heinemann.

55. Betts T (1981) Epilepsy and the mental hospital. In: *Epilepsy and Psychiatry* (ed. E Reynolds and M Trimble), pp. 175–184. Edinburgh: Churchill Livingstone.

56. Trimble M (1991) Inter-ictal psychoses of epilepsy. In: *Advances in Neurology No. 55* (ed. D Smith, D Treiman and M Trimble), pp. 143–152. New York: Raven Press.

57. Stevens J (1991) Psychosis and the temporal lobe. In: *Advances in Neurology. No 55* (ed. D Smith, D Treiman and M Trimble), pp. 79–96. New York: Raven Press.

58. Fenwick P (1995) Psychiatric disorders and epilepsy. In: *Epilepsy* (ed. A Hopkins, S Shorvon and G Cascino), 2nd edn, pp. 453–502. London: Chapman & Hall Medical.

59. Logsdail S and Toone B (1988) Post-ictal psychoses: a clinical and phenomenological description. Br J Psychiatry **152**: 246–252.

60. Trimble M (1991) *The Psychoses of Epilepsy*. New York: Raven Press.

61. Tizard B (1962) The personality of epileptics. *Psychol Bull* **59**: 196–210.

62. Schwartz J (1996) The social apraxia of epilepsy. In: *Psychological Disturbances in Epilepsy* (ed. J Sackellares and S Berent), pp. 159–170. Boston: Butterworth-Heinemann.

63. Barzack P, Edmunds E, and Betts T (1988) Hypomania following complex partial seizures. *Br J Psychiatry* **152**: 137–139.

64. Tandon R and DeQuardo J (1996) Psychoses and epilepsy. In: *Psychological Disturbances in Epilepsy* (ed. J Sackellares and S Berent), pp. 171–189. Boston: Butterworth-Heinemann.

65. Brown S and Vaughan M (1998) Dementia in epileptic patients. In: *Behaviour and Cognitive Function* (ed. M Trimble and E Reynolds), pp. 177–185. Chichester: John Wiley.

66. Betts T and Boden S (1991) Pseudoseizures. In: *Women and Epilepsy* (ed. M Trimble), pp. 243–59. Chichester: John Wiley & Sons.

67. Betts T (1997a) Psychiatric aspects of non epileptic seizures. In: *Epilepsy: A Comprehensive Textbook* (ed. J Engel and T Pedley). Philadelphia: Lippincott–Raven.

68. Lempert T, Bauer N and Schmidt D (1994) Syncope: a videometric analysis of 56 episodes of transient cerebral hypoxia. *Ann Neurol* **36**: 233–237.

69. Jehu D (1991) Post traumatic stress reactions among adults molested as children. *Sex Marital Therapy* **63**: 227–243.

70. Andermann F (1993) Non epileptic paroxysmal neurological events. In: *Non-epileptic Seizures* (ed. A Rowan and J Gates), pp. 111–121. Boston: Butterworth-Heinemann.

71. Betts T and Duffy N (1993) Non-epileptic attack disorder (pseudo seizures) and sexual abuse: a review. In: *Pseudo Epileptic Seizures* (ed. L Gram, S Johannessen, P Osterman and M Sillanpää), pp. 55–65. Petersfield: Wrightson Biomedical Publishing.

72. Cartmill A and Betts T (1992) Seizure behaviour in a patient with post traumatic stress disorder following rape. Notes on the aetiology of 'pseudo seizures'. *Seizure* **1**: 33–36.

73. Silberman E, Post R, Nurnberger J *et al* (1985) Transient sensory, cognitive and affective phenomena in affective illness: a comparison with complex partial epilepsy. *Br J Psychiatry* **146**: 181–189.

74. Treiman D (1991) Psychobiology of ictal aggression. In: *Advances in Neurology No. 55 Neurobehavioural Problems in Epilepsy* (ed. D Smith, D Treiman and M Trimble), pp. 341–356. New York: Raven Press.

75. Kinsbourne M (1964) Hiatus hernia with contortions of the neck. *Lancet* **1**: 1058–1061.

76. Mahowald M and Schenk C (1993) Parasomnia purgatory: the epileptic / non epileptic parasomnia interface. In: *Non-epileptic seizures* (ed. A Rowan and J Gates), pp. 123–142. Boston: Butterworth-Heinemann.

77. Greig E and Betts T (1992) Epileptic seizures induced by sexual abuse: pathogenic and pathoplastic factors. *Seizure* **1**: 269–274.

78. Roy A (1979) Hysterical seizures. *Arch Neurol* **36**: 447–451.

79. Betts T (1997b) Relationship between psychiatry and neurology in clinical practice (psychosomatic illness and hysteria). In: *Care of the Common Neurological Illnesses* (ed. A Williams). Oxford: Oxford University Press.

80. Ford C (1993) Somatization and non epileptic seizures. In: *Non-epileptic Seizures* (ed. A Rowan and J Gates), pp. 153–164. Boston: Butterworth-Heinemann.

81. Betts T (1997c) Conversion disorders. In: *Epilepsy: A Comprehensive Textbook* (ed. J Engel and T Pedley). Philadelphia: Lippincott–Raven.

82. Howell S, Owen L and Chadwick D (1989) Pseudo status epilepticus. *Quart J Med* **71**: 507–519.

83. Anderson J and McKane J (1996) Münchausen syndrome by proxy. *Br J Hosp Med* **56**: 43–45.

84. Kanner A et al (1990) Supplementary motor seizures mimicking pseudo seizures: some clinical differences. *Neurology* **40**:1404–1407.

85. Slater J, Brown M, Jacobs W and Ramsey R (1995) Induction of pseudo seizures with intravenous saline placebo. *Epilepsia* **36**: 580–585.

86. Derry P and McLachlan R (1996) The MMPI-2 as an adjunct to the diagnosis of pseudo seizures. *Seizure* **5**: 35–40.

Index